Andy Griffiths is t[illegible] short stories, the B[illegible] He has had a lifelong interest in health and fitness and trained with Jim Thomson for two years. He exercises every morning, tries to avoid food with labels and takes his daughter to the park most afternoons. For more information, visit Andy's website at www.andygriffiths.com.au.

Jim Thomson was born in Scotland and first came to Australia as a professional athlete. He went on to win three Australian sprint titles and broke the world professional records for 100 metres and 90 metres. In 1987 Jim was voted Australian Athlete, Male Athlete and Sprint Athlete of the Year. Jim has worked as a personal trainer and been involved in the management of leisure centres and personal training studios for over twenty years, as well as acting as a fitness advisor to the Tasmanian Institute of Sport. Jim currently owns and runs Williamstown Health and Fitness centre in Melbourne.

Sophie Blackmore is a dietician and registered nurse who holds a Bachelor of Science, with a major in nutrition, and a Graduate Diploma in dietetics. Sophie has worked in Darwin, New York and Melbourne. Her first book, *Nourish: Food for your baby*, was published in 2004. Sophie is currently working as a dietician and lives with her three sons and partner in Melbourne.

Also by Andy Griffiths
(Illustrated by Terry Denton)

Just Tricking!
Just Annoying!
Just Stupid!
Just Crazy!
Just Disgusting!
The Bad Book

And by Andy Griffiths

The Day My Bum Went Psycho
Zombie Bums from Uranus

Also by Sophie Blackmore

Nourish: Food for your baby

Fast Food and No Play Make Jack a Fat Boy

ANDY GRIFFITHS,
JIM THOMSON
and SOPHIE BLACKMORE

PAN
Pan Macmillan Australia

All care has been taken to provide accurate, safe information, but it is impossible to cover every situation, so please consult a competent health professional whenever you are in doubt about your health, or that of your child. It is also advised that you seek medical advice before embarking on any new exercise regime. The authors and publishers cannot accept legal responsibility for any problems arising out of the contents of this book.

First published 2005 in Pan by Pan Macmillan Australia Pty Limited
St Martins Tower, 31 Market Street, Sydney

National Library of Australia
Cataloguing-in-Publication data:

Griffiths, Andy, 1961– .
Fast food and no play make Jack a fat boy: creating a healthier lifestyle for you and your children.

ISBN 0 330 42180 8.

1. Children – Health and hygiene – Australia. 2. Children – Australia – Nutrition. 3. Health promotion – Australia. I. Thomson, Jim (Jim William), 1956– . II. Blackmore, Sophie. III. Title.

649.3

Typeset in 12.5/16pt Stempel Garamond and 10/16 Syntax by
Midland Typesetters, Maryborough, Victoria
Illustrations by Terry Denton
Internal design by Deborah Parry Graphics
Printed in Australia by McPherson's Printing Group

Acknowledgements

This book is the result of a team effort and would not have been possible without the encouragement, expert help and advice of Tom Gilliatt, Brianne Tunnicliffe, Jill Griffiths, Karen Ward, Mary Verney, Anyez Lindop, Louise Wills and Ian Smith.

They say we're in the middle of an obesity epidemic. An epidemic – like it is polio. Like we'll be telling our grandkids about it one day. The Great Obesity Epidemic of 2004.

'How'd you get through it, Grandpa?'

'Oh, it was horrible, Johnny, there was cheesecake and pork chops everywhere.'

– *Lazyboy*

Contents

PART 3: THE PROGRAM – PHASE ONE

PART 4: THE PROGRAM – PHASE TWO

PART 5: A DAY IN JACK'S NEW LIFE

Part 1

A Day in the Life of Jack

1. Waking up: Eat this now!

I wake up and look at the clock.

Oh no!

I've overslept . . . again!

I turn on the TV. A Chockers ad comes on. A whole load of people are eating Chockers bars and having a giant party.

Great! *Giant Fighting Robot Man* hasn't started yet. I'm in time after all.

The Chockers ad finishes and another ad starts. A lifesaver is running along the beach. He dives into the surf and catches a wave back to shore. Now he's riding a bike. Now he's back in the surf paddling a kayak with his huge arms. Now he's sitting down eating a big bowl full of cereal.

Hmmm. I've been eating that stuff for my whole

life but I still don't look like that guy. But it doesn't really matter, I guess. I don't like swimming much anyway.

Puffing slightly, I push myself up onto my elbow, grab a box of Dino cookies that I got from Craig's Burgersaurus party on the weekend and get comfortable.

I put one into my mouth and start sucking. Mmmm.

An ad for Hot Wheels cars comes on. This is followed by an ad for the new healthy menu at Burgersaurus. *As if*. Who are they trying to kid? As if anyone in their right mind would choose rabbit food over a Burgersaurus-Rex. That's not what you go to Burgersaurus for. You go for the hamburgers. And the toys, of course.

I reach over the side of the bed and pick up the Giant Fighting Robot Man action figurine with snapping arm action that I got yesterday. Well, it *had* snapping arm action. It broke ten minutes after I got it. But ten minutes is pretty good for a Burgersaurus toy. And they *are* free.

There's a sharp blast of music.

For a moment I think it's *Giant Fighting Robot Man*, but it's not. It's the new Cheesy Chunks ad. I love this song! I start singing but I have to stop because bits of cookie are going everywhere and I don't want Mum to know that I've been eating in bed.

Suddenly Giant Fighting Robot Man fills the screen.

Finally!

I put a handful of cookies in my mouth, settle back and smile.

I love this show.

A study of 13 OECD countries showed that Australia had the highest number of television food advertisements (12 per hour) in children's programming . . . The vast majority of food advertisements were for pre-sugared breakfast cereals, soft-drinks, confectionery, savoury snacks or fast food outlets. Overall, products advertised to children were considered unhealthy and contradicted recommendations for healthy eating.

– CFAC (Coalition on Food Advertising to Children), 'Children's Health or Corporate Wealth'

Australian children are exposed to the highest rate of television advertising in the world. On average, that adds up to more than 130 food ads per week. Eighty per cent of these advertisements are for food that is highly processed, fatty and sugary or salty. These are foods that could generally be considered junk.

Through the use of slim, happy children, TV food advertising creates an overwhelming message that these junk foods are cool and fun. Young children do not have the knowledge or the maturity to realise that they should not be eating these foods every day. Food advertising is highly sophisticated as it works by realising the power children have in applying pressure on parents to buy the products. And it works – the top ten fast-food chains spent $82.2 million on advertising in Australia in 2003, with McDonald's spending $26.8 million and KFC $22.6 million.

Action 1.1
Strategies to limit the influence of TV advertising

- Place a limit on the amount of television your children watch. The less television they watch, the fewer ads they will see. Obesity is lowest among children who watch television for one hour or less a day.
- Remove TVs from children's bedrooms. (See Action 4.2, 'Guidelines and hints for workable television budgeting' on page 172.)
- Place the television in an out-of-the-way position.
- Try to watch non-commercial TV or DVDs.
- Watch some of the ads. Discuss with your children how ads are designed to make you want to buy the products they advertise, e.g. they appeal to our desire for fun, to be attractive, to be strong.
- Record programs and then fast-forward through the ads.
- Be an effective role model. Show that you control the TV and not vice versa.

2.
Breakfast: Enduro-boy

I go to the kitchen cupboard and look for some cereal.

Chockoes – nup.

Rainbow Rocks – nup.

Enduro-crunch – yep. It's a new box and there's a free extreme sports DVD inside.

I open the box and pull out the DVD. It's a skateboarding one. Cool. It will give me something to watch while I eat breakfast. I slip the DVD into the computer and press 'play'.

I pour out a bowl full of Enduro-crunch. I add milk, sit down, put a big spoonful into my mouth and watch the computer screen.

But something's not right. What is it? I stare at the bowl.

Of course! I forgot the sugar.

I get the sugar bowl and sprinkle a spoonful over the Enduro-crunch. I take another mouthful. That's better.

On the screen these madmen are skating off gutters, stair rails and whole flights of stairs. I wish I could do that. But there's not much chance of that. I'm not allowed to have a skateboard. Too dangerous, Mum says.

I'm still hungry. I help myself to another bowl of Enduro-crunch. I can feel myself getting stronger and fitter with each mouthful.

Mum rushes into the kitchen.

'Hi, Jack,' she says, barely pausing as she heads towards the kettle.

'Hi, Mum,' I say. 'Can I get a skateboard?'

'No, Jack,' says Mum. 'We've been through this.'

'I just . . .' I say.

'No,' says Mum firmly. 'Now get dressed and get ready for school. We don't have much time.'

I put the Enduro-crunch away and while I'm at it I notice the Toaster Treats. I want a Toaster Treat. I pull a Toaster Treat out of the box.

'You'll have to buy your lunch today,' says Mum, handing me a five-dollar note. 'I haven't got time to make anything this morning.'

I shrug and nod. Like she ever has time to make anything. But every morning she says the same thing. And every day I buy my lunch. 'Okay,' I say.

'Something healthy,' says Mum, taking a handful of Enduro-crunch out of the box as she leaves the room, her coffee cup in her other hand.

'Yes, Mum,' I say.

The Toaster Treat is making me thirsty.

I open the fridge and pull out the fruit drink. I drink a big glass, finish my Toaster Treat and watch the skateboarding. Two of the madmen are racing each other in a long concrete drainage channel. I wonder what their mums would say if they could see them now.

'Jack!' says Mum, coming back in. 'Come on! You haven't moved!'

'I was watching the DVD,' I say.

'Well turn it off and get ready,' says Mum. 'And don't forget to take something for morning tea.'

I nod and go to the cupboard.

There is a packet of Koala Bix and two packets of Chockalots. I grab four Koala Bix and put them in my pyjama pocket. That's for morning tea. I grab one of the packets of Chockalots and put them down my pants. They're for emergencies.

Back in my room I put the Koala Bix in my school bag and hide the Chockalots in my Lego block box on top of the wardrobe.

Always be prepared: that's my motto.

Figures from the Australian Bureau of Statistics show the average Australian is eating almost 44 kilograms of sugar per year, increasing the risk of diabetes, heart disease, obesity and early death. Some manufactured and low-fat foods are filled with 'hidden' sugar but children's cereals, sports and soft drinks are among the major culprits.

– Herald Sun, *24 October 2004*

Often in our rush to pack as much into our days as possible, we neglect to feed our bodies as well as we should. It's easy to fall into the trap of relying on over-processed convenience foods that can be prepared quickly. But these are high in sugar and low in the nutrients that are essential to a sense of vitality and wellbeing. Unfortunately, many breakfast cereals marketed to children are either too sugary, too salty or lacking in fibre. A nourishing breakfast provides water and nutrients to our body and brain. While sugary processed foods provide a sudden boost to energy levels, the effect is short-lived and can result in restlessness, boredom and an inability to focus one to two hours later. Foods that are digested slowly give a slower, more even release of energy and tend to be more sustaining, which results in an improved ability to concentrate. These foods tend to be fresh, unprocessed foods. A child who has a good breakfast is more likely to be able to concentrate in class.

Action 1.2
Healthy breakfast ideas

- Healthy alternatives to highly processed breakfast foods:
  - Replace processed breakfast cereal with milk with a bowl of porridge or bran or puffed corn with skimmed milk
  - Replace muesli bars with a bowl of untoasted muesli with skimmed milk
  - Replace white toast and jam with wholemeal toast and peanut butter, Vegemite, cream cheese or avocado
  - Replace fruit drink with freshly squeezed juice or water
  - Replace fruit bars with a piece of fresh fruit or fruit salad and low-fat yoghurt
  - Replace fried eggs and bacon on white toast with a vegetable omelette and brown rice.
- Don't try to make all these changes at once. Introduce one small change every few weeks. See Action 4.6, 'Planning for a fresh food home' on page 195.
- Children are much more likely to eat breakfast if they see a parent eating breakfast.
- If you are not hungry in the morning, reduce the size of your evening meal and finish eating at least two hours before bedtime. This should lead to an increased appetite in the morning.

3. Driving to school: In the land of the fat

'Come on, Jack!' yells Mum over the combined racket of the washing machine, the clothes drier and the dishwasher. 'We'll be late!'

'Okay, okay,' I yell, grabbing my bag.

I haven't brushed my teeth or my hair, but when Mum's like this you don't argue with her.

I walk down the stairs to the garage and jump into the car. Mum presses the remote and the Roll-A-Door opens. She backs out and takes off like a Formula One driver. At the end of the driveway she jams on the brakes. A cyclist swerves around us and makes a violent hand gesture.

'Same to you, pal,' says Mum, shaking her head grimly as she pulls out onto the road. 'Honestly, these people . . .'

I nod. I guess it's not a good time to ask for a bike. Like skateboards, Mum thinks they're too dangerous.

We pass the park. The swing is still broken and there's a circle of red tape around the seesaw. It's been like that for months now.

'Can we have the radio on?' I ask.

'Sure,' says Mum, concentrating on changing lanes to get us out from behind a delivery van with a big hot dog on the roof.

I turn the radio on and hear the Chicken Shack song, and as if by magic, we pass a Chicken Shack. There's a billboard out the front advertising a whole bucket of fried chicken for $9.99. Bargain!

'Can we have Chicken Shack for dinner tonight?' I ask Mum.

'You'll have to speak to your father,' says Mum. 'He's cooking dinner tonight.'

'Cooking?' I say. 'He never cooks!'

'Well, he's in charge of dinner, anyway,' says Mum. 'I won't be home until later. So you'll have to walk home tonight, all right?'

'Walk?' I say. 'But it's such a long way! Can't I get a skateboard?'

'When you're a bit older,' says Mum.

'Why not now?' I say.

'Too dangerous,' says Mum. 'Besides, the exercise will do you good.'

'Skateboards give you exercise, too,' I say.

'Sure, until you get run over,' says Mum, swerving around another cyclist. 'It's for your own good, Jack.'

I shrug.

The radio announces that Lotza Pizza! gives you a free giant garlic bread roll with every pizza, and if you don't get your pizza delivered within half an hour of ordering it, you get a free pizza. Now that's value. The decision about what to have for dinner just got harder.

I see a picture of the new giant-sized can of Zap! lemonade on the side of a bus with the words 'Twice as many bubbles in a can twice as big!' plastered over it. Actually I *am* a bit thirsty.

We pass a billboard that shows a bunch of laughing people splashing each other with water and drinking Zap! We pass another billboard showing a double-decker hamburger, a huge container of Zap! and a mountain of French fries. Mmmmm. I could go a double-decker hamburger, a huge container of Zap! and a mountain of French fries.

As if reading my mind, Mum pulls in to a service station.

'Can I get something to eat?' I say, looking inside at the rows of well-stocked fridges, shelves of chips, chocolate bars, lollies, donuts and hot dogs.

'You just had breakfast,' says Mum, unbuckling her seatbelt. 'How can you possibly be hungry?'

'I can't help it,' I say. 'I'm a growing boy.'

Mum shakes her head and opens the door. 'Your stomach must be a bottomless pit, Jack.'

She closes the door, takes the hose from the bowser and starts filling up the car. I get out as well.

'Well?' I say. 'Can I?'

'All right,' says Mum. 'Just one thing, though.'

'Thanks, Mum!' I say.

Back on the road I'm eating a bag of potato chips. It was a two-for-two-dollars deal so I've got one for later as well. It worked out at only 40 cents extra for the second packet, so it made sense. And I've got a new Giant Fighting Robot Man disc, as well. I've already got this one, but I should be able to swap it for a Giant Fighting Robot Monster and then I'll be pretty close to having the whole set.

Over the past century especially, technology has almost completely removed physical exercise from the day-to-day lives of many people in the developed world. At the same time, it has filled supermarket shelves with inexpensive, good-tasting food that is packed with calories. And, finally, technology has

allowed advertisers to deliver constant messages that say 'Eat this now' to everyone old enough to watch TV.

– Time, *28 June 2004*

We are moving less and eating more than ever before in history: a perfect combination to create overweight adults and children. Currently 60 per cent of Australia's adult population and 25 per cent of Australian children are overweight or obese. Increased car use, lack of bike paths, not enough parks, shrinking backyards, the creation of vast suburbs where walking to shops and schools is not an option, decreased PE and sport time in primary and secondary schools and the increase in sedentary pastimes such as television viewing and electronic games all contribute to this unhealthy lifestyle. Add to this a general saturation of food advertising and exhortations to EAT NOW and you have a recipe for disaster.

Action 1.3
Easy ways to increase the amount of movement in your day

- Walk or cycle whenever possible.
- If you have to drive a car, park a few blocks away from your destination and build a five- to ten-minute walk into your day. Accumulating exercise in small bursts is as effective as one longer session for burning calories.

- If catching public transport, get off a stop or two earlier and walk the rest of the way.
- Get up half an hour earlier three days a week and go for a brisk 30-minute walk. If this is not possible, try to do a 30-minute walk at lunchtime. Or, even better, do both.
- Organise a group of friends or neighbours to go walking with early in the morning or at night.
- Take the stairs rather than the lift.

4. Before school: Computer golf

As we turn the corner into the road where my school is, Mum's knuckles tense white on the steering wheel.

There are cars and kids everywhere.

Ed the lollipop man waves but Mum's not waving. She's focused on one thing and one thing only: getting a parking spot as close as possible to the front gate.

Her eyes narrow.

She peers forward.

'Come on!' she pleads with the 4WD stopped in the middle of the road in front of us as the kids pile out of it. 'That's not a parking spot!'

'I could get out here, Mum,' I say.

'No,' says Mum. 'It's not safe.'

'But those kids are getting out,' I say.

'That doesn't make it right,' says Mum as the last kid slams the door and the 4WD moves forwards. 'Finally!'

And at the same moment the indicator on the car parked in Mum's desired spot blinks on and the car pulls out and away.

Mum shoots our car into the space.

Right outside the front gate.

'Good one, Mum,' I say.

'Thanks,' she says proudly. 'Now Jack, don't forget you're walking home tonight.'

'Can I get a snack on the way home?' I say, hoping she's forgotten about the chips.

Mum reaches into her purse and gives me two dollars. She's forgotten about the chips. 'Something healthy,' she says.

'Yes, Mum,' I say, slipping the coin into my pocket and hoisting my bag out of the back seat. 'See ya!'

I slam the car door and head for the school gate.

A game of cricket is in progress on the asphalt. Dean slams it for a four. The ball skids to a stop beside me.

'Hey, Jack,' says Gavin. 'Can you get that?'

I throw it back. They keep playing and ignore me. I'm no good at cricket. They know that. And I know that. Even if I did play they would just want me to make up the numbers. I know how it would go. I wouldn't get a bat. I wouldn't get a bowl. I'd end up on the outfield just standing there bored out of my brain.

I climb the stairs into the main building, puffing slightly with the effort. My bag's really heavy.

I go into the classroom.

Jeremy's playing golf already.

I go over to the computer. He's about to tee off to the tiny flag located on a cliff top. 'Careful,' I say. 'Too much and you'll end up in the water.'

'Tell me something I don't know,' says Jeremy, slouching in his chair with a bored look on his face. He's obviously been here for some time.

He tees off.

Thwack.

Plop.

His ball ends up in the water.

'That's the sixth time in a row!' he says, shaking his head.

'Too much force,' I say. 'Wind it back to about half and try again.'

Jeremy does as I suggest. The ball lands safely on the green beside the flag.

'Hey,' he says. 'Good advice.'

'Practice makes perfect,' I shrug. 'Wanna play doubles?'

'Sure,' he says.

I sit down next to him as he finishes putting. The chips crackle in my pocket. I pull out the bag and open them. 'Cool!' I say, spotting the disc on top. 'Giant Fighting Robot Man!'

'Cool,' says Jeremy, helping himself to a handful of chips and pushing the keyboard towards me. 'You tee off.'

'Fore!' I yell, spraying chips all over the screen as the ball flies in a graceful electronic arc down the fairway.

We laugh.

I love a round of golf before school.

We can all eat food when we aren't feeling physically hungry. This sort of eating can be called non-hungry eating. Non-hungry eating can include things like overeating, grazing, picking, nibbling and bingeing. Non-hungry eating can occur at any time, such as when we eat our main meals, in between main meals and even overnight. Many people do a significant amount of this sort of eating – certainly enough to upset their eating balance and to be a big factor in causing weight gain and difficulty in maintaining a comfortable weight.

– *Dr Rick Kausman,* If Not Dieting, Then What?

We eat for many reasons – and only one of these is to do with hunger. Humans evolved eating a variety of foods depending on what was available. We hunted and gathered. Food may have been scarce at times and it made sense to eat as much as possible when it was available – particularly foods high in fat and sugar. These provided a concentrated form of energy and would have helped our ancestors tide themselves over in leaner times.

The problem is that in the West we have created a situation in which energy-dense foods are plentiful and cheap but it is difficult for us to switch off our instinct to feast. Therefore we regularly take on more energy than we use, the balance of which is converted to fat and stored in our bodies.

Apart from availability, there are many other situations which can cause us to eat when we aren't actually hungry. We may eat if we are tired, hoping that the food will give us some energy. We may eat if we are upset, hoping that the food will give us comfort. We may also eat out of boredom, habit or because it is associated with some other activity (e.g. eating popcorn at the movies). For whatever reason, it's very easy to become swamped by both external and internal forces that are largely unrelated to hunger and be unaware of what our bodies are really telling us.

Action 1.4
Some questions to ask yourself before eating

- Am I thirsty? Am I confusing hunger with thirst? When was the last time I had a drink?
- Am I tired? Do I feel like I need a kick-start? When was the last time I moved for a few minutes?
- Am I eating out of habit? Am I engaged in another activity and not even aware of what I'm putting into my mouth?
- Am I eating because somebody just put a piece of cake in my hand and I don't want to offend them by not eating it?
- Am I upset? Is food giving me a nurturing, cared-for feeling?

5.
In class: Maths Brain challenge Part 1

One hour later we're sitting in groups of four playing Mr Fitzgerald's weekly 'Maths Brain' challenge.

I hate Mr Fitzgerald's Maths Brain challenges, because if there's one thing I don't have, it's a maths brain.

Now if he ran 'Giant Fighting Robot Brain' challenges or 'Computer Golf Brain' challenges I reckon I'd beat everyone hands down.

But he doesn't.

And what makes it worse is that each member of the winning team gets to choose a mini chocolate bar from Mr Fitzgerald's box.

And what makes it even worse still is that I'm in a group with Jeremy, Alice and Sophie, none of whom possesses a maths brain either.

And what makes it triply worse is that lunch is still more than an hour away.

'All right,' announces Mr Fitzgerald. 'Listen carefully. The pizza was cut into twelve even pieces. Betty ate one-third of the pizza. Dave ate two-sixths. Brenda ate one-quarter. How many pieces were left for John? You have three minutes to work it out. Go!'

I look around. Most of the other groups immediately start talking and writing and working out the problem. All except our group. Alice and Sophie are discussing last night's episode of *Idol*. Jeremy is staring blankly out the window. And I'm ripping small pieces of paper out of my exercise book, putting them into my mouth and turning them into spitballs.

Uh-oh.

Here comes Mr Fitzgerald.

I nudge Jeremy. 'So,' I say, trying to sound intelligent. 'What do you think John's share is?'

Jeremy stares at me blankly. 'Share of what?' he says.

'Pizza!' I say.

'I love pizza,' he says.

Mr Fitzgerald is hovering on the edge of the group, frowning. 'How are you going?' he says.

'Good,' I say.

'Well,' he says. 'How much pizza does John get?'

'Um,' I say, looking at the rest of the group who are all looking blankly at me, 'I'd say he should get a quarter.'

'Maybe that's what he *should* get,' says Mr Fitzgerald, 'but if Betty has already got a third, Dave's got two-sixths and Brenda's got a quarter, he's not going to be able to get it, is he?'

'No,' I say, shaking my head as if I understand everything that he's saying to me. 'I suppose not.'

'So?' says Mr Fitzgerald.

'So Betty should give some of her pizza to John,' says Jeremy. 'It's not fair if she gets more.'

Mr Fitzgerald takes a deep breath. 'No, it's not fair, but I'm asking you to work out how much John gets if she doesn't give him any more.'

'What sort of pizza is it?' says Sophie.

'It doesn't matter what sort of pizza it is,' says Mr Fitzgerald.

'Yes it does,' says Alice, 'because if it's got chillies I can't eat it. I'm allergic to chillies. They make my throat swell up.'

'Then you shouldn't have any,' says Mr Fitzgerald, sighing. 'But how much does John get? That's the question.'

'Is John allergic to chillies?' says Alice, but Mr Fitzgerald has already moved on.

I feel a wet sting on the back of my neck.

I turn around. Dean is trying to hide a smirk.

'You'll be sorry you did that,' I say, reaching for a spitball and loading it into my pen.

I wait for a few moments, and then I take a deep breath, spin around and blow the spitball as hard as I can at Dean's head.

Bullseye.

It hits him right in the cheek. He jerks back with such force that he falls off his seat.

Crash.

Mr Fitzgerald wheels around. 'Dean!' he says sharply. 'Get back into your seat!'

'It's not my fault,' Dean says, pointing at me. 'Jack blew a spitball at me!'

Before I can explain that Dean started it, Mr Fitzgerald turns on me. 'I would have thought that you had more important things to do.'

'Yes,' I say, 'but . . .'

'No excuses!' says Mr Fitzgerald, holding out his hand. 'Give me that pen!'

'Uh-oh,' whispers Dean. 'Fatman's in trouble.'

I ignore him, stand up, walk to Mr Fitzgerald and put the empty pen casing in his hand.

'Thank you,' he says. 'Now sit down. And concentrate!'

'Yes, sir,' I say.

I walk back to my table.

Dean is puffing his cheeks out at me.

I hate Dean.

I look at the clock on the back wall.

Still *ages* till lunch.

And, judging by the blank faces of Jeremy, Alice and Sophie, not even the faint possibility of one of Mr Fitzgerald's chocolate bars to tide me over. I hope John chokes to death on his stupid pizza.

Thanks to advances in brain research, we now know that most of the brain is activated during physical activity – much more so than when doing seat work. In fact, according to Eric Jensen (author of numerous books on brain-based learning), sitting for more than ten minutes at a stretch 'reduces our awareness of physical and emotional sensations and increases fatigue'. He tells us this results in reduced concentration and, in children, most likely discipline problems. Movement, on the other hand, increases the capacity of blood vessels (and possibly even their number), allowing for the delivery of oxygen, water and glucose ('brain food') to the brain. And this can't help optimising the brain's performance!

Rae Pica, Your Active Child

Our brains are not separate from our bodies – there is a direct link between fitness and intelligence. For example, Rae Pica reports that one French study found that children who spent eight hours a week in physical education demonstrated better academic performance, greater independence and more maturity than students with only 40 minutes of PE a week.

One of the most powerful things for both your child's physical and mental development is to ensure that they are getting a minimum of 60 minutes of exercise a day.

Action 1.5
Active bodies, active minds

- Academic achievement is not separate from physical achievement. Look for ways to encourage a balance between the two in your child's life.
- Your example is far more powerful than anything you can say. A lecture on active living delivered from the couch will have little effect.
- A child's attitude towards physical exercise will not necessarily be positive. See it as one of your essential parental roles to help them understand the benefits and experience the enjoyment of regular movement.
- Start while your child is young. Make time for a daily trip to the park.
- Give birthday and Christmas presents that encourage movement, e.g. balls, Frisbees, kites. Make birthday parties active.

- See Action 4.11, 'Alternatives to "conventional" exercise' on page 221 and Action 5.7, 'Simple resources for encouraging inside play' on page 268.

6.
Lunchtime: Pie, Zap! and Chockers

The bell finally rings for lunch.

I squeeze out from behind the desk and practically run for the canteen. I say 'practically' because I can't really run. Well, I can run, but it's not very comfortable. And I've got a sore knee, which doesn't help.

The combined smell of hot pies, pasties, donuts and chips hits me like a wave as I walk into the covered canteen area. I begin to feel close to alive again after the boring torture of trying to figure out a make-believe character's portion of make-believe pizza. An ocean of *real* food stretches in front of me. I join the shortest line and finger the five-dollar bill in my pocket. I know exactly what I'm going to get. A pie and a donut. And a can of

Zap! That will leave me enough for an ice-cream afterwards.

'Next,' says the canteen lady.

I'm about to give my order when I hear my mother's voice inside my head: 'Buy something healthy.'

I look at the hot trays steaming up the glass in front of me. Up the other end of the counter is a small bowl of wrinkled apples and spotty bananas.

'One pie with sauce . . .' I say, 'and a pineapple donut please.' Pineapple is healthy. Mum would be proud of me if she were here.

'That the lot, love?' says the woman.

'And a can of Zap!' I say, handing her the five dollars.

She gives me the food and one dollar fifty change.

I wander down the far end of the canteen where there are a few tables, but they're already taken so I head back towards the library.

The pie tastes good. The donut is even better.

The Zap! is cold.

As I walk I pass a group of kids from my class.

'Have you seen Mr Smith?' they say.

'No,' I say. I'll be seeing him soon enough, though. In fact, a lot sooner than I'd like. Mr Smith is the PE teacher. 'Why do you want him?'

'We need him to unlock the sports room,' says

David. 'We want to get a ball. And he's the only one with the key.'

'But we've got PE after lunch,' I say.

'So?' says David, not sure of my point. For some reason that I'll never understand, some kids actually *like* PE. David is one of them. There's no use reasoning with these people. They're crazy.

'Forget it,' I say. 'I'll let him know you're looking for him.'

I wander for a while as I finish my donut. Jeremy's probably already at the library. They've got the new Doom-master game. We're almost at level three. I'd really like to get there, but we can't eat in the library and I really feel like an ice-cream. I head back to the canteen, passing David and the others on the way. They're still looking for Mr Smith.

I stand at the canteen looking at the ice-cream ads.

It's a tough choice.

There are ten different types. But my budget makes the choice easier. And Mum did want me to eat something healthy. Maybe a strawberry ice-cream. Strawberries are healthy.

I'm about to order it when I notice that they've got Chockers. Chockers is the new chocolate bar covered with full-cream chocolate and nuts over a honey-almond nougat centre. I saw it on TV this morning. Nuts are healthy. And if you get a special wrapper you get a free bar!

There's no contest. Chockers it is.

I unwrap the bar as I walk. The foil glitters gold in the sun as I realise it's my lucky day.

I got a lucky wrapper!

I quickly eat the bar and go back to the canteen for my prize, which I eat as I hurry towards the library.

On the way I pass David and the others playing soccer. They obviously found Mr Smith.

I make tracks for the library. Lunch is already half over and I haven't even played Doom-master yet.

We're feeding our kids junk. And then we wonder why they can't learn, why they can't pay attention, why they're gaining so much weight. We act like it's a shock! I mean wake up! Look at what's going on here!

– *Morgan Spurlock,* Inpress, *2 June 2004*

Schools can play a powerful role in helping students to understand the relationship between food, exercise and health. Physical health and nutritional awareness should not be seen as optional extras or nudged out in favour of more 'academic' subjects. They are essential to a student's short- and long-term physical and mental wellbeing, as well as crucial in assisting them to achieve their academic potential. By providing a routine that includes time for work, movement and healthy eating, schools can play an important part in preparing a child for a lifetime of wellness.

Action 1.6
How schools can help

- Encourage children to sit down in class and take time to eat lunch together before they go outside.
- Encourage children to play outside for at least the first half of lunchtime, and all of recess.
- Ensure access to a range of areas for different outside activities, e.g. level ground, shade, climbing equipment, a sand pit.
- Review the range of food that is available from the school canteen. Restrict or completely remove calorie-dense, low-nutrient foods from the menu.
- Use nutrition and exercise units in the curriculum to back up the school strategy on nutrition and exercise. Encourage children to continue exploring these subjects and to see body education as an ongoing part of their lives.
- Provide support and encouragement for teachers to be positive role models for students in areas of nutrition and exercise.

7. PE class: I hate sport!

'What are you doing, Jack?' screams David. 'You're meant to catch it!'

'I tried to!' I pant. 'But you threw it too hard.'

'Don't call for it if you don't want it!' he says.

'I *didn't* call for it,' I say.

'Well don't just stand there,' says Dean. 'Go and get it.'

I shake my head, still trying to catch my breath. Unsuccessfully. My chest feels like it's full of cotton wool.

I'm wheezing.

I'm hot.

I'm tired.

My T-shirt is drenched.

I feel sick.

And my knee hurts.

Basketball sucks.

The basketball has disappeared into a spiky bush at the side of the court. I lie down on my stomach and reach into the prickles to get it out. As I'm getting it out a large thorn rips my arm.

Great.

Now I'm not just sweaty. I've got blood all over me as well.

Mr Smith comes over. 'What's going on, boys? Why aren't you playing?'

'Fatman lost the ball,' says Gavin.

'I didn't lose it,' I say, throwing the ball as hard as I can at his head. 'There!'

Gavin catches the ball with ease and laughs.

'Steady, Jack!' says Mr Smith. 'That's not how you pass the ball to a team-mate.'

'I'm not his mate,' I say.

'You can say that again,' says Gavin.

'That may be,' says Mr Smith, 'but you're on the same team and you're going to have to learn to get along. That's what being in a team is all about. Now shake hands and get playing.'

I look at Gavin.

I don't want to shake hands with him any more than he wants to shake hands with me.

But Mr Smith is watching and we have to.

Gavin fixes me with a look of hatred, takes my

hand for the barest minimum of time to qualify for a shake and practically throws it towards the ground.

Mr Smith nods. He returns the ball to the centre and throws it into the air. 'Play!' he yells.

Incredibly, the ball is knocked straight to me.

This time I catch it, but I've still got no idea what to do with it. The other four members of the team are screaming at me to throw it to each of them, but while I'm trying to decide, the ball is knocked out of my hand. I give chase but it's no use. I'm too slow. The other team quickly passes the ball up the court and scores a goal.

'Idiot!' hisses David as the players in the other team high-five each other. 'Why didn't you throw it to me?'

I shrug. 'I dunno,' I say. '*Everyone* was calling for it!'

'But I was the closest,' he says.

I shrug again. Basketball is not like Doom-master. I know what to do in Doom-master. If there's a sword in my hand I kill people with it. If there's a gun in my hand I shoot people with it. Come to think of it, basketball would be vastly improved if we were allowed to have swords and guns. We could all just kill each other and get it over with much faster.

I'm pondering this improvement to the game

when I look up and see Gavin, Dean and Jeremy running towards me.

It's the last thing I see before I end up flat on my back looking at the sky. The clouds look nice today. All fluffy, like massive white explosions. They are replaced by Mr Smith's head looking down at me.

'Are you all right, Jack?' he says, helping me to my feet.

'No,' I say groggily. 'Not really.'

'What's the matter?' he says.

'I feel sick,' I say. 'And I've got a sore knee.'

'Your knee's *still* sore?' says Mr Smith. 'Have you been to the doctor?'

'No,' I say.

'Jack,' says Mr Smith, 'for all I know this may be true, but you've always got some excuse. Now you can sit out for the rest of the class, but I'm going to have to ring your parents and suggest they get your knee looked at.'

'Okay,' I say, heading for the bench. I can deal with the phone call later. Right now all I want is a rest.

We recently looked at the evolution of fitness in Australian children and compared it with that of

children from 37 countries around the world. Australian children sat at No. 27 when overall fitness was measured . . . The primary recommendation from our study is that kids be encouraged to move. It doesn't matter what they do or for how long as long as they're doing something active.

– *Grant Tomkinson, lecturer,* Sunday Life, *4 July 2004*

Many overweight children have negative attitudes towards physical education. They are often last to be picked for teams. They can be self-conscious about being seen in sports gear. Because carrying extra weight reduces their endurance they are unable to keep up with their friends, overheat quickly and find exertion uncomfortable. This can lead to a vicious circle of avoiding physical activity, which leads to increased unfitness, which in turn leads to more avoidance. As a result they are less likely to develop the skills of whatever particular game is being played and accordingly derive less enjoyment from it and less motivation to improve.

Action 1.7
Encouraging children to move

- Find an activity that they enjoy, e.g. swimming, bike-riding, bowling, throwing a Frisbee, soccer, football, catch, tennis, chasey, tree-climbing, dancing, water fights.
- Effective activities are those that the child can participate in at their own level. The emphasis should be on keeping the

child moving, rather than on competition and skills acquisition.

- Join in with them – children enjoy spending time with their parents.
- Offer plenty of encouragement and advice if requested, but refrain from being critical. Children are more likely to embrace an activity with enthusiasm if they know that there's no penalty for getting it 'wrong'. If you think about it, exactly the same goes for adults.
- Kids love to rise to a challenge. You can create small challenges within any activity. For instance, in the playground you can create a mini-circuit for your child to complete by simply telling them to swing across the monkey bars, climb a ladder, come down the slide, do ten swings, climb back up the slide, down the ladder and back across the monkey bars. Challenge them to complete the circuit five times. But remember to keep it light and keep it fun. The minute it starts to seem like work, stop. Your aim is to get them to enjoy movement, not merely endure it.
- Set achievable mini-goals. For instance, five consecutive basketball hoops, three straight kicks, completing a 100-metre sprint in a certain time.
- Make a regular time each day – or each week – for a particular activity so that it becomes something children look forward to.

8.
After school: Snack attack

On the way home, Jeremy catches me up.

'How are you feeling?' he says.

'Pretty good, considering,' I say, kicking a large clod of dirt. 'Wanna come to my house?'

'I don't know,' says Jeremy. 'I should be getting home.'

'I've got PlayStation,' I say. 'With Formula One.'

'Okay,' says Jeremy. 'I'll ring Mum from your place.'

'Cool,' I say, kicking another piece of dirt. It skids off down the footpath, almost all the way to the shop. 'Let's get a sludge-ice.'

'I've only got a dollar,' says Jeremy.

'Don't worry about it,' I say. 'I've got money.'

We have enough for two medium-sized sludgeices with the bonus lollipop deal. But if you fill them right, you can get a large for the price of a medium.

We're standing at the machine and I'm showing Jeremy how to curl the top of the sludge-ice high above the lip of the container when a large blob of red sludge-ice falls onto the floor.

The guy behind the counter looks over and frowns. 'That's enough in there,' he says. 'Don't get it on the floor.'

I shrug.

What does he expect?

If he doesn't want sludge-ice on the floor of his shop then he should get rid of the sludge-ice machine.

At the register we dig around in the lollipop barrel. We eventually find the last two strawberry lollipops. The man frowns at our overfilled containers, but gives them to us for the medium price.

Back at home we are barrelling around the track at over 200 kilometres per hour but we keep crashing because the sun is streaming in onto the television screen.

'Can you shut the curtains?' says Jeremy. 'I can't see a thing.'

'Me neither,' I say, pulling the curtains across

the window. 'It's very dangerous to drive a car at 200 kilometres an hour when you can't see properly.'

The room is now dark and cool.

We sit hunched over the controls in front of the television. We don't talk much, just race. The only sounds for the next hour and a half are the whine of the cars and our lollipops occasionally clicking against our teeth.

'Yes!' says Jeremy, passing me on a tight corner.

'You'll pay for that,' I say.

'No way!' says Jeremy.

I regain the lead on an even tighter corner. 'Way!'

Jeremy's car develops serious steering problems. 'Uh-oh,' he says.

Wheels on fire, he pulls in for a pit stop.

'See ya!' I say, streaking ahead. 'Heh-heh-heh!'

But I'm too busy laughing at Jeremy to notice my car heading off the track.

'Oh no!' I yell as it crashes into a brick wall and explodes at 220 kilometres per hour. A piece of the debris shears off and smashes into Jeremy's car.

'Darn,' he says as his car plunges off a bridge and sinks beneath the water below. 'I'd better go,' he says, looking at his watch.

'Okay,' I say as my new car squeals off the starting line. 'See ya!'

'Bye,' says Jeremy, letting himself out.

My shoulders and back are hurting from all the hunching, but I want to try to get around the track one more time without crashing, before Dad comes home.

But I hope he gets home soon.

I go into the kitchen, get a packet of Tangs and sit back down in front of the screen.

Non-core foods are on average twice as high in energy as core foods and drinks. But new research shows Australian children's diets today comprise 42 per cent non-core foods and beverages, triple the recommended levels.

– Herald Sun, *23 February 2005*

Parents cannot expect children to eat enough at three meals to meet their daily nutritional needs. Kids need at least one high-quality snack drawn from core foods (water, bread, vegetables, fruit, dairy foods and meat) to keep them going until the next meal. The word 'snack', however, is often analogous with non-core foods such as sweet biscuits, chips, ice-cream and highly processed packaged single-serve snack packs. These processed foods often contain large amounts of fat and sugar and/or salt with few other nutrients.

Ideally, a snack should be a small, simple meal, providing a mixture of carbohydrate and protein. If possible, try to include something fresh. Good sources of carbohydrates include wholemeal breads, fruits, vegetables, rice and pasta. Good sources of protein include meat, eggs, milk, nuts, peanut butter, baked beans and chickpeas. If you're thirsty, plain water is the best possible drink. Sweetened drinks, including juice, contain large amounts of concentrated sugar. They are not only expensive but they can ruin a child's appetite so that they don't eat properly at mealtimes. Cutting out sweet drinks is one of the easiest and most effective ways for both adults and children to lose excess fat.

Action 1.8
Replacing junk snacks with healthy alternatives

Below is a list of common snack items containing high amounts of empty calories in the form of fat and/or sugar, and suggested healthier replacements. Don't try to make these changes all at once, however. Make one small change every few weeks and give your family time to get used to the first change before introducing the next. Trying to introduce healthier eating habits too quickly will only invite rebellion and negativity.

- Replace fruit juice, cordial, soft drinks and flavoured milk with water or plain milk. Keep a jug of water within easy reach at all times.
- Replace slurpees with smoothies made from fresh fruit, yoghurt and crushed ice. A smoothie-maker is an excellent investment.

- Replace sweet biscuits with rice cakes or wholemeal dry biscuits. Buy sweet biscuits only when needed for special occasions. If they're not in the cupboard, they can't be eaten.
- Replace potato chips with plain home-cooked popcorn or raw vegetable sticks. Keep some cut-up vegetables in the fridge, e.g. carrot, cucumber, capsicum, celery. These can be eaten plain or with a healthy dip.
- Replace fruit bars, lollies and chocolate with fresh fruit. Keep a bowl of fresh fruit within easy reach. Smaller children tend to eat fruit more readily if it is cut up and presented on a plate, or even put on skewers and toothpicks. Make it fun.
- Replace ice blocks and ice-cream with low fat yoghurt. Add fresh fruit or crushed nuts.
- See Action 3.7, 'Healthy lunch box ideas' on page 133 for more healthy eating ideas.

9.
Dad's dinner: Burgersaurus

Dad arrives home an hour later, carrying three bags and a cardboard drink tray. I can smell hot fries and fresh hamburger.

Cool! He's been to Burgersaurus!

Although I've eaten almost a whole packet of Tangs, I'm always up for Burgersaurus.

'Hi, Dad!' I say.

'Hi, Jack,' he says, putting all the food down on the coffee table. 'Dinner is served.'

'Just in time,' I say. 'I was so hungry I was about to eat the couch.'

'No need for that,' says Dad, opening the top of one of the bags with a flourish. 'Caveman Deal, *with* toy, and a Tyrannoshake!'

'How did you know that that is *exactly* what I wanted?' I say.

'Because that's what you always have,' he chuckles. 'I'll be right with you.'

He puts his briefcase down, loosens his tie and goes through to the kitchen. He returns with an open can of beer and flops down onto the couch.

'Ahhh,' he says, picking up the remote and pointing it at the television. 'That's better.'

An ad for Lotza Pizza! appears on the screen.

Followed by an ad for Chockers.

Followed by an ad for Zap!

We sit and eat in silence.

The news comes back on. Apart from the usual gloomy stuff there's an item about how Burgersaurus is bringing out an exercise video featuring Ug the caveman. There is a brief clip of the world-famous caveman doing star jumps.

Dad laughs. 'Go, Ug!' he chuckles.

After dinner Dad and I are watching the Friday night footy.

Well, technically speaking *I* am watching the Friday night footy.

Dad is asleep on the couch. On his large belly the can of beer he's clutching is rising and falling as he snores. There are two more cans of beer on the coffee table beside him, as well as the bags, wrappers and drink cups from our meal. I guess I should clean them up before Mum gets home.

My team kicks a goal. The crowd roars. Dad stirs.

Dad used to play football. He was pretty good, too. Not in the professional league or anything, but he was best and fairest a couple of years in a row.

He doesn't play anymore, though.

I really should clean up the mess.

Suddenly the living room is filled with light.

Uh-oh.

Too late.

Mum swings her car into the driveway.

I jump up to try to get rid of it all, but I knock a large cup of Zap! off the coffee table and it splashes everywhere. I'm staring at the soggy fries on the carpet when Mum walks in.

Crunch.

Mum bends down and picks up the splinters of what was a white plastic spoon. The noise causes Dad to stir.

He belches, adjusts himself and rolls over.

The can of beer falls from his hand and tips all over the front of his pants.

He quickly sits up.

'Darn it!' he says. He eases his legs over the side of the couch. With difficulty.

Mum raises a hand to her mouth to stifle a giggle.

Dad looks up, a dopey expression on his face.

'Oh, hi,' he says.

'Good game?' she says, nodding towards the television.

'I don't know,' he says. 'I think so. Must have fallen asleep.'

He stands up and notices us staring at the front of his pants. 'This is not what it looks like,' he says sheepishly, blinking at us with bleary red eyes.

'I know,' says Mum, 'I saw it happen. You look wrecked.'

'I feel it,' he says.

Mum watches Dad as he stumbles from the room, knocking against the glass cabinet that holds his old football trophies.

If you eat crap food just now and then, good luck to you, but if you eat it most of the time, you have no respect for the greatest machine ever invented – YOU.

– *Dr John Tickell*, The Great Australian Diet

There are 728 McDonald's stores in Australia and they serve one million customers each day. The demand for fast food is indicative of the rushed lifestyle that has become a feature of modern life.

Fast food is relatively cheap (if you don't take into

account the long-term environmental and health costs), and requires no planning, no shopping, no cooking and no washing up. And in most cases, it doesn't even require you to get out of your car. It is reliable and predictable: you know exactly what you are getting, no matter what city or country you're in, which appeals to the often conservative and unadventurous nature of children's tastes. And if you do venture out of your car, in many cases there are even playgrounds for the children.

So what is the problem with fast food? The problem is that highly processed energy-dense foods dominate the menu. The core menu items of fast-food stores include high amounts of saturated fat, sugar, salt and caffeine. The human body is unable to regulate the intake of energy-dense fast foods: by the time we feel full, we have eaten way too much. Then, strangely, one and a half to two hours after eating fast food it is not uncommon to feel tired or lethargic – a feeling which some people may associate with hunger . . . Twenty-four to 48 hours later the energy in food that is not used to fuel movement is converted to fat and stored in the body.

Action 1.9
Ways to cut down on fast food

- Do not rely on fast food as a matter of routine. Reduce visits to fast-food restaurants to no more than a few times a year.

- Limit the amount of food bought – choose regular serves over large.
- Drink water rather than non-thirst-quenching soft drinks.
- Serve a range of interesting foods with a variety of tastes at home so that children learn to become more adventurous with their tastes.
- Plan ahead. Try to always have a supply of fresh fruit, wholemeal breads, raw unsalted nuts and water available.
- Don't use fast-food restaurants as places to celebrate such things as birthdays or end-of-season break-ups. It teaches children to associate good feelings with junk food. This type of association can be very powerful, and very difficult to 'unlearn' later in life.
- Learning more about fast food can seriously reduce your appetite for it. The documentary *Supersize Me* is entertainingly shocking and may well put you off eating burgers and fries for life. There are also some great books on the fast-food industry, which could have the same effect. See the recommended books list in the Sources and resources section on page 294.

10. Bedtime: Tight pyjamas

I finish cleaning up the rest of the takeaway meal.

'How was your day, Jack?' says Mum, pouring herself a glass of wine.

'Good,' I say, trying to push the rubbish into the bin. The bin is pretty full already with the wrappers and containers from last night's dinner, but I manage to push it all down tightly enough to get the lid to stay on. 'How was yours?'

'Busy!' she says, looking at the clock. 'Time you should be getting to bed. You look tired.'

'I don't *feel* tired,' I lie.

'Don't argue with me, Jack,' says Mum. 'I haven't got the energy.'

'But the game hasn't finished yet,' I say.

'Record the rest of it and watch it tomorrow,' says Mum.

'But what about *Giant Fighting Robot Man*?' I say.

'What about him?' says Mum.

'When will I watch that if I'm trying to watch football?' I say. 'And tomorrow is *Survivor* as well. And don't forget *Who Wants to be a Millionaire?*'

Mum sighs and hangs her head. 'Maybe you'll have to choose what you want to watch most,' she suggests.

'Are you crazy?' I say. 'How can I choose? If I don't watch *Survivor*, how am I ever going to learn to survive in the wild? And how am I going to improve my general knowledge if I don't watch *Who Wants to be a Millionaire?* Unless you don't care about that. Unless you want me to grow up to be dumb. Or to be eaten by crocodiles.'

Mum smiles wearily. 'I can assure you that I don't want either of those things,' she says. 'But neither do I want you to be tired for school tomorrow.'

'But it's Saturday tomorrow!' I say. 'There is no school.'

'Oh,' says Mum. 'I forgot. I suppose you can stay up till the end of the match then.'

'Thanks, Mum!' I say.

'But put your pyjamas on first,' she says.

I go down the hallway to my room and get my pyjamas out. They're Zap! pyjamas. I got them by saving up the barcodes off Zap! packets, but that was a while ago and they're getting tight.

I'm still trying to get the top button on the pants done up as I walk back into the lounge room.

Mum looks at me. 'Are they getting too small for you already, Jack?' she says.

'No,' I say, quickly pulling the top down. 'They're okay.'

But before I can get out of the room, Mum comes over and inspects them.

'You need the next size up,' she says. 'Sizes are never right for kids. They certainly don't allow for puppy fat.'

'You think I'm fat?' I say.

'No,' she says quickly. 'I said *puppy* fat. You're a growing boy. Just getting ready for the next growth spurt, I'd say,' she says.

'But you think I'm fat at the moment,' I say.

'No!' says Mum, even more strongly.

A bit too strongly.

'Jack,' says Mum. 'Are you getting enough exercise?'

'Yes,' I say.

'You spend half your time in front of the TV and the other half in front of the computer,' says Mum. 'When do you get all this exercise, exactly?'

Hmmm. That's a hard one. But not impossible. 'At school,' I say. 'In PE.'

Mum looks sceptical. 'Jack,' says Mum, 'your PE teacher rang me today. He said you've been complaining about a sore knee and spend most PE periods in the library. Is that right?'

Ouch. Sprung. 'Yes,' I admit.

'Then I'll take you to the doctor next week,' says Mum.

'Um,' I say, 'we don't have to do that. It's not *that* sore.'

'Either you have a sore knee or you don't, Jack,' says Mum. 'And I'm sure Dr Lee will be able to tell us.'

I nod. That's exactly what I'm afraid of.

Anyone can spot a really obese child, but for many kids it's hard to say whether or not they are overweight just by looking at them in the playground or the street. Maybe this is because we're all getting fatter . . . One in four school-age children are overweight so most don't stand out these days – especially when half of all adults are overweight, too. When children are 20 kg overweight they're obese and they stand out, but when they're 5 kg overweight it's not nearly so obvious. So we're not picking up the borderline overweight kids who have the greatest chance of recovering.

– Associate Professor Melissa Wake

As a population, Australian adults are getting fatter. Children who are overweight often grow up to become overweight adults, with all the associated health problems that carrying excess fat causes. We need to be aware of excess fat on our children but also recognise that every person has a different weight and body shape.

There is no perfect weight for a child. Children grow and their weight and fat stores are changing continuously. A child who feels they are overweight may be embarrassed about their shape. Teasing or negative comments about physical appearance can contribute to low self-esteem, which can contribute to not wanting to change their health and lifestyle. Ensuring that children have a healthy lifestyle and healthy self-esteem is more important than worrying about the shape of their body. If we look after our lifestyle and self-esteem, our bodies will naturally evolve into their own healthiest shape.

Action 1.10
Five ways to help your children feel good about themselves

- Don't attach too much importance to physical appearance. Do not let them hear you criticising your own body – or anybody else's. Talk about other positive aspects of a person: skills, personality, etc.
- Come down firmly on teasing. It is not harmless. It can have very damaging short- and long-term consequences

on the self-esteem and self-image of the person being teased.

- Encourage your child to find a special interest (apart from TV-watching and playing computer games) that they enjoy and are good at.
- Question media that promotes unrealistic and unhealthy body shapes. Limit your – and your child's – exposure to it.
- Keep a family scrapbook in which the achievements, highlights, photographs and comments of each family member are recorded. As it builds it provides a positive reinforcement both for the individuals and the identity of the family.

Part 2

Wake-up Call

1.

Supermarket Part 1: Wandering and whining

Saturday morning.

We are circling the car park of our local supermarket. We have been around three times now.

'There's a park, Mum,' I say.

'Not close enough,' says Mum.

We drive slowly along the row.

'There's one!' I say.

'Still not close enough,' says Mum.

I nod.

Finally Mum finds a park about ten spaces from the entrance. 'This will have to do,' she says.

We pick up a trolley that insists on listing to the right at every chance and start wandering down the first aisle. There is a huge pyramid of twelve-can

Supa-saver boxes of Zap! with a 'TWO FOR $10.99' sign attached. 'Can we get some, Mum?' I say.

'Do we need that much Zap!?' says Mum.

'Yes,' I say. 'Especially at that price.'

'Okay,' sighs Mum.

I put two boxes in the trolley and we wander on.

Half an hour later the trolley is full.

Chips, Cheesy Chunks, a value box of twelve mini ice-creams, toilet paper, a bottle of red cordial, fruit drink packs, four packs of Tangs, dishwashing detergent, ice-cream, milk, cream, Chockoes, Rainbow Rocks, Enduro-crunch, dog food, Chockalots, Koala Bix, Delights, white bread, Fruties, croissants, batteries, Danish pastries, bacon, frozen crinkle-cut chips, frozen meat pies, Toaster Treats, rubber gloves, frozen sausage rolls, frozen chicken nuggets, sausages, fried noodles, instant noodles and a tub of coleslaw.

On the way to the checkout we pass the self-serve lollies.

'Can I have a bag of lollies, Mum?' I beg. 'Please?'

'No, Jack,' says Mum. 'We've got enough.'

'Please?' I say. 'I'm *so* hungry!'

'We'll be home soon,' says Mum.

'I'll be dead by then,' I say. 'And it will be all your fault.'

'Don't do this, Jack,' says Mum.

'Just let me have some lollies and I won't,' I say. 'I promise.'

'No,' says Mum, pushing the trolley up to the checkout. There are small refrigerators at the end of each aisle with cold bottles of Zap! Mum is reading a glossy magazine that features a movie star on the front and the words 'Miranda's miracle cabbage soup diet!'

'Can I have a Zap! Mum?' I say. 'I'm thirsty.'

'No,' says Mum. 'We've already got some.'

'But it's not cold,' I say. 'And it's really hot outside.'

'No,' says Mum.

'But I didn't get any lollies,' I say. 'Can't I at least have a Zap!?'

Mum sees that I am not going to give up and that she's not going to get any more reading done until she gives in. 'All right, Jack,' she says. 'But don't expect one every time!'

I nod and smile.

That's what she always says.

The majority are conditioned to demand and accept bland, processed, chemically treated, generally unnatural foods, which through packaging and

marketing have been made to seem wholesome. I have no doubt that any people made to eat this way would in time grow fat.

– *Mireille Guiliano,* French Women Don't Get Fat

Supermarkets provide very convenient one-stop shopping. It must be remembered, however, that supermarkets are not concerned about whether you make healthy choices.

Eighty per cent of the floor space in most supermarkets is taken up by processed, pre-packaged foods. Only 20 per cent is given over to fresh foods in their natural state. Supermarkets attempt to maximise profit by getting you to buy more than you actually need or had in mind to buy. They do this by using many tricks to influence what you buy and how much of it you buy. Staple products such as milk, bread and meat are separated, thus forcing you to wander around the supermarket where you – and your children – will be tempted into buying products that you had not intended to buy. Items that appeal to children, such as brightly packaged, sugary biscuits and cereal boxes, are placed at a child's eye level. Lollies and chocolates are positioned at the checkouts. 'Special' signs and two-for-one promotions attract attention, but on close inspection the special may not be such a saving. Becoming aware of how a supermarket is laid out for the benefit of the supermarket rather than the customers is the first step to becoming more in control of what you buy and why.

Action 2.1
Five ways to save money – and your sanity – at the supermarket

- Make a shopping list at home. Take it with you and buy only what is on the list. Get in and get out. Don't wander.
- Shop for fresh fruit and vegetables first. Aim to fill at least 80 per cent of your trolley with fresh, unprocessed or minimally processed foods before you shop for the processed.
- Don't go shopping when you're hungry or in a bad mood.
- Whenever possible, leave the children at home. There's no need to make it any more difficult than it already is.
- Consider ordering groceries over the internet. The delivery fee will probably be less than the money you save by not impulse-buying needless items.

2.
At the footy: Monkey see, monkey do

'You little white maggot!' yells Dad over the top of the roaring crowd.

'One-eyed trouser snake!' yells his friend Bill.

'Idiot!' I yell.

I look up at the scoreboard.

Carlton is trailing by six points.

And according to my dad and Bill, and at least half of the crowd, it's all the umpire's fault. The poor guy. Even though I barrack for Collingwood, I feel kind of sorry for him. He doesn't seem to be able to please anyone this afternoon.

I pull my duffle coat tighter against the wind.

Davis takes a screamer right in front of the goals and the crowd goes mad. Dad and Bill salute 'cheers' to each other with their plastic cups of beer.

'It's in the bag!' yells Dad, his top lip white with beer foam.

Davis puts the ball down on the ground. He pulls up his socks. He picks up the ball, walks back and boots the ball through the goalposts.

The crowd erupts.

The siren wails.

Half-time.

That's good. That means hot pies, hot chips and Zap!

'Did you see that?' says Bill, elbowing me. 'Did you see that? He reminds me of your father, that guy.'

'Get out of here,' says Dad.

'Don't underestimate yourself,' says Bill. He turns to me. 'I remember once your dad took a mark just like that one. They were five points down and there was one minute to go before the final siren. But he wasn't in the goal square. He was down the other end of the field. But you know what? He ran the entire length of the field and kicked a goal. I'd never seen anything like it. And I haven't seen anything like it since.'

'Is that true, Dad?' I say.

'Bill says it is,' says Dad, draining the last mouthful of beer from his cup. 'But it was a long time ago.'

'Why did you stop playing?' I ask.

'Injuries,' says Dad. 'I guess I got too old.'

'That's too bad,' I say. 'I wish I'd seen you play.'

'Just look at Davis,' says Bill. 'That's your dad. Reincarnated.'

'Knock it off, Bill,' says Dad. 'I'm not dead yet. And anyway, I was never that good.'

'You knock it off!' says Bill. 'You were one of the best.'

'So you keep saying,' says Dad.

Bill gives up on Dad and turns to me again. 'So, Jack,' he says. 'How's your footy going?'

I shrug. 'Not so good,' I say.

'What do you mean, "not so good"?' he says. 'You don't like footy?'

'I like it all right,' I say. 'I just don't like playing it.'

'He just needs a bit more practice,' says Dad.

Bill nods. 'Well,' he says to me, pointing at Dad. 'You've got a good coach there. You listen to him.'

'Sure,' I say, nodding.

'Let's go get some food,' says Dad, standing up.

To look at him with his big stomach and solid build you wouldn't think he'd been a champion, but like he says, it was a long time ago.

Before I was born.

We walk down to the food kiosks.

There's a big crowd. But it's warmer than sitting in the grandstand and it smells good. Dad gives me a twenty and he and Bill go off to get beer.

I buy three pies, a can of Zap! and a bucket of hot chips. I push the end of the sauce bottle deep into each of the pies and squeeze until tomato sauce oozes out of the pie edges. I sprinkle extra salt on the chips, put everything in a cardboard tray and go back to our seats. Dad and Bill are already back, drinking beer and deep in an analysis of the second quarter.

I give them their pies, sit down and watch the Little League match going on in the centre of the ground. The little kids are kicking a ball marked with a big red B in the middle. Burgersaurus.

On the scoreboard there's an ad for Lotza Pizza!

Pizzas are good, but nothing beats a pie at the footy.

Well, nothing except for hot chips, maybe.

I crack open my can of Zap!

I love footy.

Parents need to realise that if they eat out three or four times a week and don't exercise, they're gonna raise kids who eat out three or four times a week and don't exercise. They have to lead by example.

– *Morgan Spurlock,* Inpress, *2 June 2004*

Children learn by copying. The rhythms and routines of your life become the rhythms and routines of theirs. If you are not eating properly and not exercising regularly, they will copy that too. As a parent, you are the most powerful influence in attitudes, including those of activity and food choice. Parents who spend time shopping, preparing and eating food are showing their children the enjoyment they get from food. Parents who enjoy activity are more likely to have a child who sees activity as a normal and pleasurable part of life. Studies have shown that if one parent exercises, a child is twice as likely to exercise. If both parents exercise, then their child is *six* times as likely to exercise. Clearly, actions speak much louder than words or exhortations to be healthier. Any significant lifestyle change for the child needs to come first from the parents.

Action 2.2
Five ways to be a healthy role model for your children

- Let them see you making – and taking – time to exercise and to be active. Don't assume that because you haven't exercised for twenty years, it's too late to start now. It's never too late. An improvement in your – and your children's – health is available immediately.
- Let them see you eating slowly and enjoying a range of fresh, unprocessed foods.
- Let them see you enjoying cooking and meal presentation, and involving them in the process.

- Let them see you switching the television on to watch a program that you really want to watch and then when it's finished, switching it off.
- Let them see you enjoying a balance between work, family and play and having time for them and the truly important things in life.

3.
Barbecue dinner: Where there's smoke there's burnt sausages

When we get home I'm starving. 'What's for dinner?' I say.

'I bought some sausages,' says Mum. 'I thought we'd have a barbecue.'

'Great idea,' says Dad. 'I'll cook.'

'Good,' says Mum. 'I'll make the salad.'

She opens the fridge and pulls out the tub of coleslaw that she bought at the supermarket this morning, despite me telling her that I don't like coleslaw.

She plonks the salad into a glass bowl. White strips covered in a thick creamy paste.

I was right.

I still don't like it.

In fact I like it even less.

'Here,' says Dad, handing me the plate of snags. 'Can you carry these? My hands are full.'

I tear my gaze away from the hideous dripping salad and see that Dad is wearing his comedy apron with the hairy chest and big boobs. It's only slightly less horrible than the coleslaw. He's holding a can of beer in one hand and a pair of barbecue tongs and a fork in the other. 'Let the barbecuing begin!' he says.

I follow him outside.

He lights the barbecue and scrapes a thick layer of white gunk from the top of the plate. He flicks it onto the grass.

'Yuck,' I say, 'that's gross.'

'Better out than in,' says Dad. 'That's the great thing about barbecues. They're healthy!'

That's weird. I wouldn't have picked my dad as a health nut, but there you go.

The hotplate is smoking now.

Dad lays down a large wedge of butter and it sizzles noisily. He spreads it out across the plate and dumps the sausages on top.

'Run and get me another beer, would you, Jack?' says Dad, crumpling his can and handing it to me. 'This barbecuing really gives a man a thirst.'

'Sure, Dad,' I say.

I go inside to the fridge and pull out a beer for

Dad and a Zap! for me. Barbecuing gives a boy a thirst as well.

'Oh, Jack,' says Mum, handing me a packet of frozen crinkle-cut chips. 'I almost forgot these.' As I pass the pantry I grab a box of Tangs. It's just not a barbecue without Tangs.

When I return the sausages are going crazy, spitting, steaming and smoking. Dad is stabbing at them with a fork like they're trying to attack him. Which they practically are. Huge jets of hot liquid are spurting from their skins where he punctures them. I'm reminded of a documentary they showed us in school about volcanoes.

'Mum said to give you these as well,' I say, handing him the chip bag along with his beer.

'Thanks,' says Dad. He tears the top of the packet open and dumps them into the lake of boiling sausage fat, creating yet more hotplate mayhem.

We crack open our cans at the same time, nod and take a long drink each. Barbecuing is not only healthy, it's *fun*. But then, everything's more fun with Zap!

I tip a handful of Tangs into Dad's hand and grab a handful myself.

'We're almost done here,' says Dad after a few more minutes.

Smoke is pouring in thick plumes from the sausages now.

I think he's right.

I pick up the serving plate and hold it while Dad puts the blackened sausages and almost blackened chips onto it.

We take it inside and put it on the coffee table. Mum is watching the news. She puts three sausages and a handful of chips onto my plate, along with a spoonful of coleslaw.

I don't bother arguing.

I pick up the tomato sauce and squeeze it all over the top of the salad. Then I squeeze it all over the sausages. And all over the chips. And then, just in case, I squeeze it in the spaces in between the chips and the sausages and the coleslaw as well.

I don't like coleslaw.

But I *do* like tomato sauce.

The food we eat is like fuel. It gives our bodies the energy they need to function well. If you don't make sure that the fuel you pump into your body is of the right quality or quantity, you just won't feel as healthy as you could. We all have up to 100 trillion cells in our bodies, each one demanding a constant supply of daily nutrients in order to function optimally. Food affects all those cells, and by extension every aspect of our being: mood, energy

levels, food cravings, thinking capacity, sex drive, sleeping habits and general health. In short, healthy eating is the key to wellbeing.

– *Dr Gillian McKeith,* You Are What You Eat

A barbecue is a great Australian outdoor cooking experience. It can be simple or complicated, meat-based or vegetarian. As in all areas of eating, however, we need to pay attention to the quality of ingredients over their quantity, and be aware of what we are doing to the food as we prepare it. Consuming large amounts of meat soaked in fat and burnt to a crisp is not in the best interests of your body. Neither is a salad that is drenched in high-fat dressing.

Excess fat is stored in your body, gram for gram, so go for the leaner cuts. Once fat is stored, it is much harder to shift, as your body uses non-stored sources of energy first and only then starts converting stored fat to energy. So it's much better to avoid eating it in the first place.

Action 2.3
Quality versus quantity – good ideas for barbecues

- Replace large serves of sausages and fatty chops with small pieces of lean meat, chicken, fish or tofu.
- Many vegetables are delicious sliced and lightly barbecued, e.g. potato, onion, pumpkin, eggplant, zucchini, mushroom. Use a small amount of olive oil.

- Avoid pre-packaged salads drenched in oil or mayonnaise. Make your own using fresh ingredients to create a delicious salad high in nutrients and low in fat. Serve dressing separately so people can add it if they want it. Alternatively, just sprinkle salads with lemon juice.
- Avoid overcooking and/or burning food. It destroys both the flavour and much of the goodness.

4.
Footy replay: Wake-up call

'Goal!' yells Dad, raising himself up off the couch so suddenly that the packet of Delights on his stomach falls onto the floor. He points at the TV. 'Did you see that, Jack?'

'Yes,' I say, 'but I still think Wilson is better.'

'He can run, all right,' concedes Dad, picking up the packet and lying back down, 'but he can't kick.'

An ad for Atomic Blast ice-creams comes on.

'Can I have dessert?' I say.

Nobody answers.

I look across at Mum, who is sitting in her recliner rocker reading *Fast Track Your Fitness: 7 days to a new you!*

'Yes,' says Mum, looking up from her book. 'There's some ice-cream.'

'And a Toaster Treat?' I say.

Mum frowns. 'How about you have a banana instead?'

'I hate bananas,' I say, getting up and going to the kitchen.

'Don't be silly,' says Mum. 'Since when?'

'Since forever,' I say. 'Bananas are for monkeys.'

'Have you eaten any fruit today?' says Mum.

'Toaster Treats have fruit in them,' I say. 'Look!' I bring the box back into the lounge room and point at the front. 'See? Ten per cent strawberry and blueberry flavour. And it's 97 per cent fat free!'

Mum shrugs. 'That's flavouring,' she says. 'It's got nothing to do with fruit.' But she doesn't say no.

'So I can have one?' I say.

'One,' she says.

'Two?' I say.

'One,' says Mum.

'Come on,' says Dad, coming to my aid. 'He's a growing boy!'

'I'm well aware of that,' says Mum.

'So I can have two?' I say.

Mum doesn't answer me. That means yes.

I return to the lounge room with my Toaster Treats and ice-cream. The game has started again. Gary Clarke retrieves the ball and shoots through the centre with it.

'See that, Dad?' I say. 'That's what I'm talking about!'

But Dad doesn't respond.

I look across at him.

He's wincing.

'Are you okay, Dad?' I say.

He sucks his breath in hard through his teeth. 'I'm all right,' he says.

Mum looks up. 'Do you want some water?'

Dad draws his breath in sharply again, and rolls slowly off the couch, knocking the Delights onto the floor again. 'Yeah,' he says, stepping on top of the biscuits with a crunch. 'But I'll get it. Don't worry, it's nothing.'

He takes a few uncertain steps towards the door and then lurches sideways. He grabs the side of his trophy cabinet for support.

Mum launches herself out of her chair and puts her arm around him. 'Where's the pain?' she says.

'Here,' says Dad, putting his hand on his chest.

'Jack!' says Mum. 'Ring an ambulance!'

I put my bowl onto the coffee table and head for the phone.

'Don't be silly,' says Dad. 'You're overreacting.'

'You're having a heart attack!' says Mum.

Dad guffaws. 'It's not that bad. I'll be all right in a minute. My heart's fine.'

My hand hovers over the zero button. I look to Mum. 'So, should I ring?'

'Yes!' says Mum.

'No!' says Dad, wincing again. His face is white.

I press zero.

I don't want him to die.

I press it again.

He *can't* die.

I press it for a third time.

He's my dad.

I had a medical check-up recently and was told I was going to be in the grave at 60 – like my father – if I kept on eating pies and all the rubbish I did on trips away. I'm 56 tomorrow and it was a real wake-up call. I got onto the fruit and vegies, a little bit of lean meat, plenty of fish and exercise every morning and I've lost about 20 kilograms. I cannot believe the energy and how good I feel.

– *Rex Hunt,* Sunday Life, *6 March 2005*

Cardiovascular disease (CVD) is a name given to a range of diseases including heart disease and stroke. It is the number one cause of death in Australia, accounting for over 40 per cent of all deaths. It also causes illness and diminished quality of life. CVD used to be considered a disease of older people. However, increasing rates of obesity and physical inactivity in younger people mean CVD is being seen in children as young as ten. About 80 per cent of adults have at least one of the following modifiable lifestyle CVD risk factors:

- tobacco smoking;
- being overweight;
- physical inactivity;
- high blood pressure;
- high blood cholesterol;
- feeling stressed or lacking control.

The good news is that by changing lifestyle and addressing risk factors, the damage can be reversed.

Action 2.4
Five ways to reduce the risk of cardiovascular disease

- Stop smoking – or at least steadily cut down. There are many books and resource groups that can assist you in this process. Acknowledge that nicotine is a powerful addiction. Don't try to give it up all by yourself. And be prepared to have a number of attempts before you succeed.
- Make 30 minutes of moderate activity on most days of the week an absolute priority in your life. Put this book down right now and go for a 30-minute walk.
- Reduce excess weight stored around your abdomen. You can begin to do this by moving more and eating less.

- Identify an area of your life that is causing you worry. Make a list of ten things you might do to improve the situation. Even the process of making the list can make you feel better.
- Have your blood pressure and blood cholesterol checked at least once a year. NB: High blood pressure and high cholesterol have no physical symptoms, so they need to be tested. Take the time to have an annual check-up with your GP. It's much better to identify potential problems early than to discover them only after a serious health problem crops up.

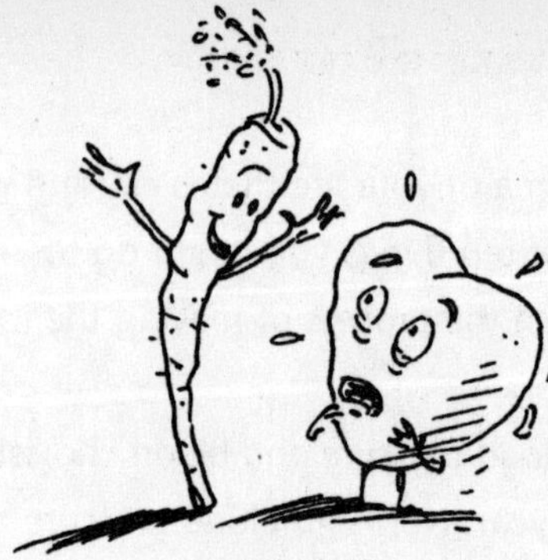

5.
Doctor's office: The good bad news

One week later we're sitting in Dr Lee's office waiting for the results of Dad's blood tests. Dr Lee is our family doctor. Mum insisted I come along as well to get my knee checked out.

Dad's pain has stopped and he's looking much better. It turns out it wasn't a heart attack after all – he got discharged from the hospital the next morning after a bad case of heartburn – but they wanted him to speak to Dr Lee.

I wish the doctor would hurry up. I'm tired. I hate it here. It smells of Pine-O-Cleen.

Finally. Dr Lee comes into the room. 'Sorry to keep you waiting,' he says.

He sits down on the other side of the desk.

'Well, Doc,' says Dad. 'How bad is it?'

The doctor raises his eyebrows as he studies the sheet of paper in his hands.

'Well,' says Dr Lee, 'as you know, you had heartburn. The blood tests and the stress test that they did at the hospital indicate that there was no damage done to your heart.'

Dad smiles and nods. 'That's good!' he says.

'Yes,' says Dr Lee, 'but these figures are not great. Your cholesterol and blood sugar levels are raised and your blood pressure is up a bit. You're not dead yet by a long shot, but you could be setting yourself up for some very serious health problems – diabetes being one of them.'

Diabetes? I don't even know what it is, but it doesn't sound good.

'Are you sure?' says Mum.

'I'm afraid so,' says the doctor.

Dad nods.

He looks at Mum. She smiles weakly.

'So, Doc, is there any good news?' says Dad. 'Can I take a pill or something?'

Dr Lee nods. 'You're young,' he says. 'I could prescribe a course of pills, but they won't be treating the root cause of the problem.'

'Which is?' says Mum.

'The combination of a lack of exercise and too much dietary fat,' says the doctor.

'But I *do* exercise,' protests Dad.

'Every day?' says the doctor.

'Yes,' says Dad.

Mum looks at Dad in surprise.

Dr Lee frowns. 'You do?' he says.

'Well,' says Dad. 'Not *every* day, of course; I've got a lot on at work at the moment and it's not always easy to find the time.'

'Once a week?' says the doctor.

Dad hesitates as he tries to recall the last time he got some serious exercise. 'Not every week, but *some* weeks . . .' he says.

'Once a month?' says the doctor.

Dad nods. 'Yes, definitely,' he says. *Most* months, anyway . . .'

'Unfortunately that's not enough,' says the doctor. 'The minimum recommended amount for an adult is 30 minutes of moderately vigorous activity.'

'Per week?' says Dad, hopefully.

'Per day!' says the doctor. 'Most days of the week.'

Dad sits there. He looks stunned.

'But I don't want to turn into some sort of pavement-pounding carrot-muncher,' he blurts. 'Besides, even if I did, it's too late now. I've left it too long.'

'Nobody said anything about eating carrots,' says the doctor. 'Although it's an excellent start.

And it's *never* too late. If you start exercising now and reducing the amount of fat in your diet you could still head a lot of these problems off at the pass.'

Dad looks sceptical. 'But my grandfather smoked and drank and didn't exercise a day in his life and he lived until 95!' he says.

The doctor nods. 'That may well be true and you are perfectly free to adopt this strategy for your own life, but you should be aware that on balance the evidence is that you won't make it to 95 and even if you do, you won't be enjoying optimum health. Being overweight and not exercising puts you at higher risk of heart attack, stroke, diabetes, high blood pressure, loss of sexual function, some cancers and depression. Of course, there are those people, like your grandfather, who for reasons of genetic or environmental good luck can beat the odds, but it's an extremely high-risk strategy for achieving wellbeing and, as your doctor and as a friend, I wouldn't advise it.'

Dad sits quietly, taking in Dr Lee's words.

'Well?' says the doctor.

'He'll try the exercise,' says Mum. 'We all will. We'll take the dog for a walk first thing in the morning.'

'Dog?' says Dad. 'I didn't know we had a dog.'

'Very funny,' says Mum. 'And speaking of

exercise, Dr Lee, I was wondering if you could take a look at Jack's knee . . .'

Modern sedentary lifestyles have created an epidemic of health risks due to lack of appropriate physical activity. It is widely recognised that physical inactivity is associated with over 30 of the most prevalent physical and mental health concerns in developed countries. The number of Australians considered at risk for disease and dysfunction due to inactivity has been estimated to be at least 44 per cent and rising. Appropriate physical activity is both prevention and antidote for disease and dysfunction associated with physical inactivity. Physical activity provides essential stimuli to develop and maintain human function, and is therefore necessary to the health and vitality of the whole person (body, mind, and spirit).

– Guiding Principles of the Bluearth Institute

In 2001 the Australian Bureau of Statistics reported that 68 per cent of Australian adults had exercise levels that were sedentary or low. This is a startling statistic, given that regular exercise combined with a sensible – but not restrictive – eating plan will guarantee you a better quality of life and ensure that you will feel even healthier, happier, smarter, more energetic and confident both now and as you grow older. Think of it as an insurance policy.

Many people are happy to take out health insurance and life insurance against the possibility of ill health or death in the future for a much greater cost than it takes to implement a simple 30-minutes-a-day exercise program. And the benefits are immediate. Whether or not you like exercise – or *think* you don't like exercise – there is no getting around the fact that to keep your body and mind functioning efficiently you need to exercise.

If you want your car to run reliably and smoothly, you would take the trouble to have it serviced regularly. Your body is no different. It needs regular care and attention, and exercise is the best way to do this. Moving improves circulation, joint flexibility and bone strength. Improved circulation helps to move nutrients to the cells and remove waste. Your belief that you don't like exercise does not change this fact. The belief that 'it is too late' is simply that – a belief. Don't let it stop you from taking the first step towards a program of increased movement. It's never too late.

Action 2.5
How to make room in your life to move

- Many people say they are 'too busy' to exercise, but on average most people spend two to three hours a day watching television. Remember, there are 168 hours in a week. You only need three to make an enormous positive difference to your health.

- Many people say they are 'too tired' to exercise. Regular exercise improves general fitness and stamina and leaves you feeling good, with more energy.
- The hardest part of starting a regular exercise program is establishing the habit. After the first month, however, once you've experienced the benefits of your increased movement, it becomes much easier and self-motivating.
- Don't think of exercise as one more thing to add to an already crowded lifestyle. Think of it as an essential foundation that makes your lifestyle possible.
- Aim to exercise for at least 30 minutes most days of the week. This can be accumulated in small amounts throughout the day if necessary. It all counts.
- Exercising in a sustained block first thing in the morning is an excellent way to ensure it doesn't get 'busied out' later in the day.

Part 3

The Program – Phase One

1. Walking the dog: All rest and no walkies make Rusty a fat dog

Dad and I are in the living room watching Formula One when Mum bustles into the room.

'When's the last time either of you took Rusty for a walk?' she says.

I look at the great pile of matted red hair lying outside the back door. Somewhere underneath it is a dog. But I haven't seen him for a while.

Dad and I both shrug.

'Well it's about time you did,' says Mum. 'He needs exercise. And so do we.'

'I don't,' I say. 'I don't like exercise.'

'Don't be silly,' says Mum.

'I'm not being silly,' I say. 'I'm telling the truth!'

'That's not the point,' says Mum. 'Whether you

like it or not, you *need* it. And so does Rusty.'

'But my knee . . .' I say.

'Oh yes, I forgot,' says Mum. 'Your mysterious sore knee which the doctor couldn't find anything wrong with and which only ever seems to get sore when someone suggests you exercise or play sport.'

'I can't help it,' I say.

Mum stands in front of me, her hands on her hips. 'Well I can,' she says.

'Mum,' I say, waving her out of the way.

'Yes?' she says, standing her ground.

'Can you move, please? I can't see the television.'

Mum glares at me. 'That's very rude, Jack.'

'Why is it rude?' I say. 'I said "*please*".'

Mum's only response is to pick up the remote and turn the TV off.

'Hey!' says Dad. 'I was watching that.'

'Me, too,' I say.

'You're *always* watching that,' says Mum. She pulls the curtains apart and daylight floods the room. 'Welcome to the day!'

'But what about the racing?' I say.

'Racing, football, golf, cricket . . .' says Mum. 'It never ends! Now what I want to know is, where is Rusty's leash? We're going for a walk!'

'I can't,' I say. '*Giant Fighting Robot Man* is on at four o'clock. A special one-hour episode.'

'Record it,' says Mum.

'I don't know how to work the timer,' I say. 'It's too complicated.'

'Then you'll either have to learn or you'll have to miss it,' says Mum. 'I'm sure you can manage without it for one afternoon.'

Great. Dad's got health problems and now Mum's lost her mind.

'I can't go either,' says Dad. 'I need to take it easy. Doctor's orders.'

'The doctor's orders were to get some exercise,' says Mum.

'But I'm still recovering!' says Dad.

'Nobody's suggesting that you do a triathlon,' says Mum. 'Just a nice slow, easy walk.'

'I will, all right?' says Dad. 'But not today.'

'If not today, then when?' says Mum.

'Tomorrow,' says Dad. 'I'll feel better tomorrow.'

'You'll feel better tomorrow because you're going to go for a walk today,' says Mum firmly. 'Now where is the leash?'

Dad and I look at each other blankly.

'We don't know,' I say. 'Too bad. It was a good idea. Can we turn the TV back on now? *Please*?'

'Get up and do it yourself,' she says, placing the remote on top of the bookshelf. 'Get at least that much exercise.'

'Fine,' says Dad. 'Can you turn the TV on, Jack?'

Exercise and a diet fortified with vitamins, fruit and vegetables helped older dogs learn new tricks and kept them spry in an experiment that scientists say could teach humans a thing or two. Beagles given the fortified diet, regular exercise or both did much better in learning new tricks than dogs fed regular chow and allowed to lie around more.

– Age, *19 January 2005*

Forty per cent of domestic Australian dogs are currently overweight. The effects of lack of exercise on a dog are boredom, back-biting, barking and increased danger of heart disease, arthritis and mental deterioration. Lack of exercise has remarkably similar effects on human beings. If you own a dog it is important to make sure that it eats a good-quality diet, and that it gets a minimum of half an hour a day exercise. If you own a body, and/or a brain, it's even more important to ensure they get at least this level of care if you want to keep them running efficiently and disease-free. Sometimes we need pets to remind us that we are animals too.

Action 3.1
Dog and human care

- Ensure your dog has a properly balanced diet. This should contain proteins to repair and build the body, carbohydrates for energy, fats to absorb and move nutrients in the body, and vitamins and minerals for body maintenance, health and to protect against disease.
- Ensure that YOU have a properly balanced diet. This should contain proteins to repair and build the body, carbohydrates for energy, fats to absorb and move nutrients in the body, and vitamins and minerals for body maintenance, health and to protect against disease.
- Exercise your dog for at least 30 minutes at least once a day. Forms of exercise can include walks, off-the-leash runs and structured play.
- Exercise your body for at least 30 minutes at least once a day. Forms of exercise can include walks, off-the-leash runs and structured play. Why not do this with your dog?
- Teach your dog new tricks to keep its brain sharp and alert.
- Teach yourself new tricks to keep your own brain sharp and alert.

2.

Supermarket Part 2: Pester power

'Do we need bread, Jack?' says Mum as I struggle with yet another supermarket trolley that's determined to go sideways instead of straight ahead.

'Yes,' I say as the trolley crashes into the bakery aisle.

Mum picks up a loaf of wholemeal bread.

I pick it out of the trolley and put it back on the shelf. 'Not that one,' I say. 'I want white.'

'But this is healthier,' says Mum.

'White tastes better,' I say. 'And if you get wholemeal I won't eat it and I'll get hungry and starve to death and that's not healthy.'

Mum sighs and picks out a loaf of white bread. 'What else do we need?'

'Tangs,' I say. 'We're down to our last box.'

'Last box?' says Mum. 'But I bought four boxes last week!'

I shrug. 'Well, they're gone.'

I wrestle the trolley down the biscuit aisle. I find the Tangs and put five boxes in the trolley.

'Do we really need five?' says Mum.

'Yes,' I say firmly. 'Unless you want to run out.'

As we walk I get more Koala Bix, more Chockalots and a new type of Delights with Irish cream flavouring.

'No,' says Mum, putting the Delights back on the shelf. 'Enough's enough, Jack.'

'But Mum,' I say, 'please, please, please?'

'No,' she says.

'Pretty please?' I say, putting the packet back in the trolley. 'With sugar on it?'

'No!' She smiles, replacing the packet on the shelf. 'We've got enough biscuits.'

'So let me get this straight,' I say. 'Are you, the best mum in the world, saying to me, the best son in the world, that I can't have one little packet of biscuits?'

'That's right,' says Mum, unmoved by my flattery.

'I bet Dad would buy them for me,' I say, putting them back in.

'I'm not your dad,' says Mum, taking them back out.

'So you're saying I can't have them?' I say.

'No,' says Mum.

She falls for my trap. 'So you're NOT saying that I can't have them?' I say. 'Thanks, Mum!' I put the biscuits back into the trolley.

'That's not what I said,' says Mum, removing the biscuits, 'and you know it!'

Drat. But it's not over yet. 'Oh, I get it,' I say, striking the side of my head with my open palm. 'What you're *really* saying is that you don't love me.'

'Now come on, Jack,' says Mum. 'I'm not saying that at all. You're putting words into my mouth.'

'Am I?' I say. 'You say that you love me, but you won't buy me what I want.'

'I do buy you what you want,' says Mum. 'And I do love you.'

'Prove it,' I say.

'I don't have to prove it,' says Mum.

'That's because you don't really love me,' I say.

'Oh for goodness' sake, Jack,' says Mum. 'Can we just move on?'

'But we haven't got the biscuits,' I say.

'We're not getting the biscuits!' says Mum.

'But Mum,' I say, putting them back in. 'Everybody's got them at school. And they're on TV.'

'For the last time,' says Mum, 'no! We don't need them and they're too expensive.'

'Fine, then,' I say, taking the biscuits out of the trolley and putting them back on the shelf myself. 'I'll go without *friends* if that's what you want.'

Mum bites her lip. 'Be reasonable, Jack,' she says.

'I am being reasonable,' I say. 'You're the one not being reasonable. You're the one who doesn't want me to have any friends! Some life I ended up with. A mother who doesn't love me and no friends.'

'Jack,' she says softly. 'I do want you to have friends. But friends who like you for who you are. Not the sort of friends who are only your friends because you're eating the same sort of biscuits as them.'

'But aren't friends people who have things in common?' I say.

'Ye-es,' says Mum uncertainly.

'Well, liking the same biscuits is something in common,' I say. 'And being able to share them. That's all. That's the only reason I wanted them. But if you think sharing is a bad thing, then fine, I don't need them.'

It's my last attempt. It's all I've got. I start to push the trolley along the aisle.

Mum shakes her head, takes the biscuits off the shelf and drops them in. I smile and look straight ahead like I haven't noticed.

We turn the corner into the confectionery aisle.
I see the Chockers bars.
'Can I have a Chockers?' I say.
'No, Jack,' says Mum.
'Please,' I say. 'Pleeeeeease?'

Years ago sociologist Vance Packard described children as 'surrogate salesmen' who had to persuade other people, usually their parents, to buy what they wanted. Marketers now use different terms to explain the intended response to their ads – such as 'leverage', 'the nudge factor', 'pester power'. The aim of most children's advertising is straightforward: get kids to nag their parents and nag them well.

– *Eric Schlosser,* Fast Food Nation

From a child's perspective a supermarket is full of brightly coloured packets and sweet and salty treats, products they are often familiar with through advertising. Many children would be happy to fill a supermarket trolley to the brim with these heavily processed foods and drinks. For parents who go shopping with young children and who are attempting to fill their trolley with more wholesome foods, the supermarket can be a challenge. For children it can be a very frustrating experience. Children may not be clear about what products are in their best interests, and they are unlikely to understand how a budget limits what and how much you can buy.

Action 3.2
Effective strategies for dealing with children in the supermarket

- Negotiate any treats prior to entering the supermarket, not while you're in there.
- Use a shopping list. Explain that you are only going to buy the items that are on your list. Talk to them about what you're buying and why.
- Involve kids in the shopping process. For instance, let them push the trolley. Give them the responsibility of making the choice between two brands of a product that's on your list. This is an ideal opportunity to teach them how to read labels and to assess manufacturers' claims.
- If your child starts nagging and pestering, make them aware of their behaviour. Talk to them about what they are doing and how it makes you feel. Don't threaten or punish as this can inflame the situation.
- Listen to your children and what they say they want, but don't feel that this means you necessarily have to buy it. It is okay to say 'no', but you have to let them know you mean it. If a child perceives weakness or hesitation, they will work on it. Remember, they have millions of years of evolution pushing them towards a preference for sugary and fatty foods. You have only your wits to rely on.

Consider a parent assertiveness training course if necessary – effective parenting requires patience, knowledge and lots of practice!

3.
Spinach dinner: I hate vegetables!

It's dinner time and I'm sitting on the couch prodding at an enormous mound of soggy green slime. 'I can't eat this,' I say.

'Why not?' says Mum.

'Because I've never seen it before, I don't know what it is, and I don't like it,' I explain patiently.

'How do you know you don't like it unless you try it?' says Mum.

'Because I only have to look at it,' I say. 'It is green. It is slimy. And it stinks.'

'You *have* to eat it,' says Mum. 'It's part of the program.'

'What program?' I say.

'Our healthier life program,' says Mum. 'Besides, it's spinach, and spinach is good for you.

Don't you want to grow up to be big and strong like Popeye?'

'Popeye!' I say. 'Who's that?'

'Popeye the sailor man,' says Mum. 'It was a cartoon. Whenever he ate a can of spinach, muscles popped out all over his body.'

I roll my eyes. If Mum thinks some lame cartoon from a million years ago is going to get me to change my mind about spinach, she's wrong. 'It was a *cartoon*,' I say. 'We're real. And this stuff is not fit for humans.'

'Just *try* it,' says Mum.

'I can't,' I say.

'What are you worried about?' says Mum. 'That you might like it?'

'That's the least of my worries,' I say.

'I love it,' says Mum.

'Then *you* eat it,' I say, offering her a big dripping forkful.

'I *am* eating it,' says Mum, putting a large amount of her own slime into her mouth.

'You're disgusting!' I say, looking across at Dad who is clowning around behind Mum's back. He's got his hand around his throat and is pretending to be sick. I giggle.

'What's so funny?' says Mum, looking around at Dad and catching him in the act. 'You know, you could at least help me,' she says.

Dad, red-faced, stops pretending to be sick. 'Eat up, Jack,' he says unconvincingly. 'It's healthy.'

'If this is healthy,' I say, 'then I'd rather be unhealthy. Anyway, it's not me who's sick, it's Dad!'

'I'm not sick,' says Dad. 'It was just a little bit of heartburn and everyone's overreacting.'

'I'm not overreacting!' says Mum. 'I'm just doing what the doctor said and trying to eat better food.'

'Spinach is not *better* food,' I say. 'It looks like it was scraped out of a drain.'

'Jack!' says Mum quietly. 'Eat it or you won't be getting any dessert.'

'Okay,' I say. 'I won't have any dessert.'

'Eat it or you can go to your room without any dinner at all!' says Mum, getting red in the face.

'Can I just eat one mouthful?' I say.

'No,' says Mum. 'All or nothing.'

'Two?' I say.

'All!' says Mum.

'I can't,' I say. 'It stinks!'

'All right,' says Mum, running out of patience. 'That does it. Go to your room!'

'But Mum . . .' I say.

'No,' says Mum.

'You can't blame him,' I hear Dad say as I walk down the hallway. 'Never could stand the stuff myself.'

'Didn't anything the doctor said to you sink in?' says Mum.

I go into my room and shut the door.

I tilt a chair hard up against the door handle.

It wasn't me who went to hospital.

I'm not sick.

I eat Enduro-crunch for breakfast every morning.

I went for a walk today.

I'm fine.

And I'm starving.

I climb up to the top of my wardrobe to my secret food box. I pull out the packet of biscuits that I 'borrowed' from the kitchen.

I flop down on my bed, turn the television on and crunch down into a good, honest, non-slimy Chockalot.

Many parents complain about the amazingly narrow and conservative range of food that most children eat. This is related to their love of routine and predictability, which, as we have seen, provide reassurance in a world that is quite complex, strange and incomprehensible.

– *Dr Reinhard W Ronnebeck,* 7000 Days

Few parents would not have experienced the frustration of having a child who eats the same limited foods to the exclusion of all else. To a child, however, the world is a strange and unpredictable place. There is so much to learn and it's so easy to get something wrong. As a result, they love familiarity and routine. And this extends to their food. The real key to getting children to eat vegetables, or any other unfamiliar food, is simply to make that food familiar.

Action 3.3
How to encourage your children to eat a wide variety of foods

- Children are more likely to eat food at mealtimes if they are hungry. Hunger is a far more effective motivation to eat dinner than parental pleading or bribery. Avoid sweet drinks or biscuits just before dinner.
- As people get older it is harder to change their 'style' of eating, or food preferences. If you ask your child what they want to eat when they are too young, they become more and more conscious of their likes and dislikes, which can cause fussiness. Give your child the family meal. The tastes and flavours of your cooking will become familiar to them. Without unnecessary choices they will happily eat it.
- Taste perception can change with time. The time taken may vary. Simple changes, e.g. whole to skimmed milk, can take one to two weeks. Bigger changes may take longer, e.g. five tastes or 30 tastes, before the food is accepted. Be patient, and simply keep presenting the food and encouraging the child to eat small amounts, without lecturing, cajoling, threatening or punishing them.

Be prepared to present the same food a number of times.

- Refrain from saying, 'Jack doesn't like spinach', even though you may think it. Children frequently change their minds. They may not like mushrooms on Monday but think they are fine on Tuesday.
- Serve different parts of the family meal in separate dishes and encourage the child to take a little from each one. This way the child can control how much of what food they put on their plate. Remember, your aim is simply to increase the child's familiarity with a particular food – the quantity eaten will increase naturally over time.
- Serve food at a table. Turn off the television. Be a good role model for your children and let them see you enjoying a wide range of the foods that you want them to eat.

4.
Jack's bedroom: Secret food stash

I'm naked.

I'm in the middle of a big pool of slime, trying desperately to keep my head above the surface.

But it's hard work.

The slime is heavy and all I have to help me is a fork.

I try to paddle my way to the edge, but it's useless.

I'm tired.

The fork is no help.

And I can hardly breathe.

Mum appears on the bank. 'Use the fork!' she yells, making an eating motion with her hand. 'Use the fork!'

Huh? I think she wants me to use the fork to eat the spinach!

But I can't.

I just can't.

And I'm going down . . .

I hear knocking.

I open my eyes, blinking against the light.

The television is blaring.

'Jack?' says Mum, from the other side of the door.

'Yes?' I say, sitting up.

'Can I come in?' she says.

'Sure,' I say, noticing the empty Chockalot packet on the floor. I quickly kick it under the bed and take the chair away from the door.

'Were you asleep?' she says.

'Um, yeah,' I say. 'I think so. I was dreaming.' I reach across and turn the TV down. 'What time is it?'

'Ten o'clock,' she says. 'I just wanted to say I'm sorry about tonight. I just want us all to be healthier. Your dad's not well. And to tell you the truth, I'm a little concerned that you're carrying more weight than is good for you.'

'So you *do* think I'm fat,' I say.

'I didn't say that,' says Mum.

'You think *I'm* going to have a heart attack?' I say.

'I didn't say that either,' says Mum. 'But I do think we need to make some changes.'

'Like eating spinach,' I say gloomily.

'And exercise,' says Mum.

'But . . .' I say. 'But . . .'

'What?' says Mum.

'I don't like sport!'

'Why not?' says Mum. 'Goodness knows you watch enough of it on TV.'

'I like *watching* it,' I say. 'But I'm no good at it. I'm too slow.'

Mum nods. 'Well, I'd like you to at least *try*,' she says. 'And take Rusty for a walk. That would be a start.'

I nod. 'Okay, Mum,' I say. 'And can I get a skateboard?'

Mum winces. 'I'll think about it,' she says. 'Perhaps if you eat your spinach . . .'

'Yes,' I say. 'I'll eat all my spinach. Besides, I learnt my lesson tonight.'

Mum smiles, gets up off the end of the bed and comes over to give me a kiss.

But as she does there's a loud crunch.

Uh-oh.

She looks down, bends over and picks up the empty Chockalot packet. She holds it in front of me and shakes her head.

'This has got to stop, Jack,' she says, dropping the packet in my wastebasket.

'Yes, Mum,' I say.

'What have you eaten today?' she says. 'Did you get a healthy sandwich?'

I shrug.

'You didn't, did you?' she says.

'No,' I say.

'Then what?' says Mum.

'A pie,' I say. I don't think she needs to know about the donut and the lemonade.

'Things are going to change,' she says.

I nod. 'They will,' I say. 'I promise.'

'So do I,' says Mum.

I don't have any problem with junk food advertisers targeting me as a parent . . . What I object to, and I think many parents do, is this heavy commercial pressure on young children who are sort of promoted to pester their parents and it exploits their credulity. I think that we have a responsibility for ourselves, but we actually also have a responsibility for our children, and I don't think they need to be exposed to this very heavy pressure.

– *Boyd Swinburn,* The World Today, *2004*

It's not an easy task to be a responsible parent in a society that promotes the overeating of calorie-dense foods as well as reducing the need for us to move. It can, of course, be done – but not all at once. As always, your greatest power as a parent is the power of example.

Action 3.4
Parent power

- Rather than worrying unduly about your child's eating and exercise habits, work on improving your own. Although it may not be immediately apparent, your example will have a subtle but powerful long-term effect on what the child comes to regard as 'normal' behaviour.
- Restrict your child's exposure to mass media advertising, whether through radio, television, newspapers, magazines or the internet.
- Try to resist labelling certain types of food as 'good' and other types as 'bad'. They all have their place in a balanced diet. Instead, teach your child the difference between foods that are eaten every day and foods that should only be eaten sometimes.
- Practise and demonstrate self-control. You have the choice about what foods to put, or not to put, into your mouth. It's not up to the food, or some other external factor, to decide. *You* decide what's right for you.
- Spend time talking with your child about their life. Resist the temptation to lecture, judge or give advice. Just listen and respond accordingly. They will be far more likely to

seek your advice and follow your example if they know that you are not going to lecture or try to persuade them to your point of view.

5.
Miracle Skywalker Part 1: Results without effort

It's late. My mouth is dry from eating all the Chockalots. I get up and go to the kitchen to get a glass of water.

Dad is still awake. He's watching TV.

'Jack!' he says. 'Come and look at this!'

I go into the living room. On the television is a muscular man with long hair. He is on a machine that looks like two skis with big lever-type handlebars. And judging by the smile on his face he's having the time of his life.

'I'm telling you,' he says without even panting despite his body being a blur of movement, 'this is the greatest piece of exercise equipment ever designed! Forget your exercise bike. Forget your running machine. This is the only piece of exercise equipment you will ever need! And the best thing is that it does the exercise for you! All you have to do is strap yourself in and hold on. While it exercises every muscle in your body you can watch TV. You can listen to music. You can ring a friend! All for less than the price of a gym membership. What are you waiting for? Ring now and the Miracle Skywalker will be yours.'

Dad puts his beer down on the coffee table and rubs his hands together. 'What do you think, Jack?' he says. 'Looks pretty good, doesn't it?'

'Yeah,' I say, rubbing my eyes.

'It does the exercise for you!' says Dad. 'You can't ask for better than that!'

'No,' I say. 'And he looks pretty fit.'

'I'm going to get one,' says Dad. 'I reckon I could get back into shape with one of those. I don't see how you couldn't.'

'Yeah,' I say. 'That's a great idea. You should get it. How much is it?'

'If I ring in the next half-hour it's 50 per cent off the normal price,' says Dad.

'What's the normal price?' I say.

'I don't know,' says Dad, reaching for the phone, 'but at 50 per cent off it's got to be a bargain. *And it does the exercise for you.*'

While Dad is ringing I continue to watch the ad.

The man is demonstrating how to use the Skywalker to exercise your arms, your legs, your abs, your shoulders, your back and even your bum. And when you get sick of going forwards, you can go in reverse!

Dad hangs up the phone and pats me on the back. 'Well, son, we are now the proud owners of a Miracle Skywalker.'

'Fantastic, Dad,' I say. 'When will it arrive?'

'Day after tomorrow,' he says. 'I paid extra to have it delivered express.'

'Wait till Mum finds out,' I say.

'Yeah,' says Dad. 'Then she'll see how serious I am about exercise. This calls for a celebration. Jack, can you get me another beer out of the fridge?'

'Sure, Dad,' I say.

He rubs his belly with his hand. 'Gotta give the Skywalker something to work with.'

Endlessly searching for an easier way, a magic bullet, miracle cure, a holy grail, is a misguided quest . . . The problem with many people is that they shy away from anything that appears to be hard work. They're always looking for short cuts. As soon as they see something that promises results 'quickly', 'easily', 'effortlessly', 'while they sleep', 'without exercise',

and so on, they whip out their wallets and take the bait, hook, line and sinker.

– *Tom Venuto,* Big Fat Lies!

Be extremely wary of exercise products that promise results without effort. They fall into the same shady area as diets that promise results without exercise. Whether they come in the form of body wraps that promise to melt fat, vibrating belts that promise to reduce flabby beer bellies to titanium-strength six-packs, or electronic fat-zappers, none of these will surpass the value of a structured long-term plan of sensible eating and exercise. The only results that most of these products will produce with minimal effort is to fatten the pockets of the snake oil salespeople who are only too happy to cater to the dreams of people desperate to believe that the energy in–energy out equation doesn't apply to them.

Action 3.5
Five questions to ask about diets and exercise equipment

1. Does it promise results with little or no effort?
2. Does it promise results in an amazingly fast time?
3. Is it expensive?
4. Is it too good to be true?
5. Is it advertised on late-night TV?

If your answer to any of the above is yes, then be afraid . . . be very afraid. But don't give up. There are many effective, low-cost ways to begin making big improvements to your health.

- Instead of starting a more active lifestyle by buying an elaborate piece of exercise equipment, resolve to make 30 minutes of movement an everyday part of your life. If that seems like too much, start with fifteen minutes, and increase the amount by five minutes each week. It's movement – and the effort you put into it – that is the key to improved muscle tone and weight loss.
- Rather than 'diet', simply try to choose foods that are in their natural state as often as possible.
- Whatever your current alcohol intake is, resolve to cut it by one drink per week. Sip a glass slowly rather than gulping it down quickly. Small, achieveable changes will make a big difference in the long run.
- If you are going to spend any money, spend it on educating yourself about nutrition and fitness. Most libraries and bookshops have a large section dedicated to this topic. Find a book that speaks to you and read it. (See the recommended list in the Sources and resources section on page 294 for some useful titles to begin with.) Make it your business to be informed about how your body works and how to ensure that it keeps working.
- Another powerful way of increasing your knowledge about how to achieve and maintain a healthy level of physical fitness is to consult an experienced personal trainer. Yes, they can be expensive, but they are a bargain compared to

an unused piece of exercise equipment, not to mention what you'll spend in the future on medical consultants attempting to fix illnesses that could be prevented with a little knowledge and effort now. Consider joining a group program or sharing the cost with a group of friends. The knowledge and experience that a good personal trainer can provide you with can save you years of frustration and/or trial and error.

6. Breakfast: The lecture

Mum is standing in the kitchen watching me as I finish my second bowl of Enduro-crunch. I'm still hungry. I reach for the box, but Mum stops me.

'Don't you think you've had enough, Jack?' she says.

'No,' I say.

'Why don't you have something else if you're still hungry?' she says.

'Why?' I say, shrugging, tipping the box. 'I like Enduro-crunch.'

'Because,' she says, taking the box out of my hand, 'if you read the label on the side, you'll see that the recommended serving size is 30 grams. In that 30 grams there are 7 grams of protein, 21 grams of carbohydrates, and 2 grams of fat.'

'Mum?' I say. 'What are you talking about?'

She picks up a book. 'It's all in *Fast Track Your Fitness*,' she says. 'Correct me if I'm wrong, but I estimate that the bowl in front of you has a capacity of roughly 60 grams and, as you are filling the bowl to capacity, this means that you are eating twice the recommended serving size. Now as you have already had two bowls, which represents a pile of Enduro-crunch four times the recommended serving size *and* you've added a cup of full-cream milk to each bowl, this brings the amount you've already eaten to an incredible 798 calories, which would take approximately three-and-a-half hours of walking to burn off, or one-and-a-quarter hours if you ran. Add to that the fact that the amount of sugar you've just consumed is equivalent to four-and-a-half tablespoons. This means your blood sugar levels will be peaking right about now and crashing in about an hour's time which will leave you feeling restless, irritable and hungry again. So I'd say you've had quite *more* than enough, wouldn't you agree?'

I look closely at Mum.

'Are you okay?' I say.

'I'm fine,' she says, removing the box from my hand and putting it at the top of the cupboard. 'From now on these are a Sunday morning treat only!'

'But what will I have for breakfast?' I say.

'Porridge,' says Mum.

'Porridge?' I say.

'Porridge,' says Mum.

'What does that have in it?' I say.

'Oatmeal,' says Mum. 'Plain 100 per cent oatmeal. You just add water for a nutritious, filling breakfast.'

'No,' I say, ignoring the fact that Mum's beginning to sound like a crazy robot. 'I mean what comes with them? A toy? A card? A DVD?'

'Nothing, as far as I know,' says Mum. 'Just oatmeal.'

'Then what's the point of that?' I say.

'Like I said,' says Mum. 'It's nutritious and filling.'

I don't know about the robot part, but she *is* crazy.

I realised that I have spent so many years being on a diet that the idea that you might actually need calories to survive has been completely wiped out of my consciousness. Have reached point where believe nutritional ideal is to eat nothing at all, and that the only reason people eat is because they are so greedy they cannot stop themselves from breaking out and ruining their diets.

– *Helen Fielding,* Bridget Jones's Diary

Eating more food than you use leads to an energy imbalance so that the excess energy is stored as fat. In an effort to lose weight, many people opt to count calories. By taking in fewer calories than they use, fat is lost. Having a general knowledge of the relative energy density of different types of food can be helpful for weight loss. Calorie-counting, however, is of limited use because everyone has a different metabolism and different energy requirements. Be wary, too, of placing too much importance on bathroom scales. Your weight can fluctuate between 1 and 2 kilograms a day depending on a number of factors. How your clothes fit you and how you feel are much more useful – and more reliable – indicators of progress.

Action 3.6
Why calorie-counting doesn't work

- Calorie-counting distracts you from the far more important issues of enjoying fresh food and moving more.
- It is impractical for most people to add up numbers all day and it's not a sustainable long-term lifestyle change.
- Different people have different metabolic rates. The exact number of calories your body requires is very difficult to determine and depends on many factors, including how active you are, your age, the temperature and your state of health.
- Healthy eating is an art, not a science. Counting calories can take the enjoyment out of food and eating. It's also easy for foods to become classified as 'good' and 'bad'.

It is more sensible to allow yourself to sample and enjoy the infinite variety of tastes and pleasures that food has to offer – but to slow down and concentrate on quality rather than quantity.

- Calorie-counting relies on numbers, rather than listening to your own body telling you when you are hungry. A little bit of a high-calorie food that you are craving may be far more satisfying – and lead to less overall calorie intake – than a lot of a low-calorie food.

7.
Lunch box: Healthy lunch ideas

'Speaking of healthy food,' says Mum, picking up a magazine, 'I've got a list of healthy lunch ideas here. Tell me what you'd like.'

Uh-oh. I'm not sure that the words 'healthy' and 'lunch' belong together. I'm more interested in the combination of the words 'edible' and 'lunch'.

I can see brightly coloured pictures of fruit and vegetables and smiling children. Not good at all.

Mum begins reading. 'How about a sweet potato and date terrine with saffron and ginger sauce and roast squab pigeon on a skewer?'

She pauses and looks at me. 'Well?'

'Um, what else is there?' I say.

'Goat cheese soufflé with sweet garlic jus on a bed of finely sliced mandarin and blood orange?'

she says. 'Or maybe some wild mushroom and yabby risotto with a salad of witlof and celeriac and a mint yoghurt dressing? Oh, no, wait – here's one! Corn-fed chicken on sweet and sour pickled pasta with artichoke, cheese and green beans! Doesn't that sound good!'

'Hmmm,' I say. 'It's all *so* tempting.'

'You can say that again,' says Mum. 'I understand it's a very difficult choice.'

She's got no idea just *how* difficult.

'Can I have the corn-fed chicken on sweet and sour pickled pasta with artichoke, cheese and green beans?' I say.

'Good choice, Jack!' she says.

'But without the artichoke or green beans?' I say. 'And white bread instead of the sweet and sour pickled pasta?'

Mum looks doubtful. It obviously doesn't say anything about this type of sandwich in her healthy lunch ideas list.

'But that's just a corn-fed chicken and cheese sandwich!' she says.

'Actually, hold the corn-fed chicken,' I say.

Mum sighs. Then she brightens. 'All right,' she says. 'But I'll put in slices of peeled apple cut in cubes with a squeeze of lemon to stop them browning. And a bottle of water. I froze the water bottle so that your lunch will stay cool.'

'Gee, thanks, Mum,' I say.
A nice cold cheese sandwich.
I should be able to swap that no problems.
When it warms up, of course.

All over the world, there are people who live longer and happier lives because they have always eaten foods that have contributed to their spectacular state of good health. Specifically, they have eaten wholefoods – unrefined foods to which nothing has been added or taken away. Essentially, wholefoods are used as close as possible to their original state. They contain no artificial colourings, preservatives or additives. Fresh vegetables and fruits are wholefoods. So too are fresh fish, poultry and meats. Dried beans, peas, lentils, rice are interesting wholefoods. These all provide valuable nutrients as well as fibre which is essential for the normal working of our digestive systems.

– *Margaret Fulton*

If you've got the time and interest to prepare elaborate lunch boxes for your children, then that's great. But you don't have to go to that much trouble. A range of simple foods in their natural form is not only nutritious but easy to prepare.

Action 3.7
Healthy lunch box ideas

One of the quickest and most effective ways to prepare a healthy sustaining lunch with minimal preparation time is to cook extra at dinner and put the leftovers in a small plastic container in the fridge. Add a piece of fruit and a bottle of water the next morning and you're done. Healthy eating is not complicated, but it does require a little planning. The list below contains some suggestions for simple healthy additions and substitutions for your child's lunch box. Choose two or more from the following list.

Cereals

- Replace white bread with multigrain, wholemeal or pita bread
- Replace two-minute noodles with fresh pasta – preferably pasta types they can eat with their fingers: ravioli, penne, tortellini, spiral
- Replace jam as a filling for sandwiches with toppings such as peanut butter or Vegemite

Fruit

- Replace fruit bars, lollies, chocolates and chips with one or two pieces of fresh fruit
- Replace roll-ups, fruit bars and muesli bars with a handful of nuts and/or dried fruit. Try making a simple homemade muesli slice with rolled oats, sultanas, sunflower seeds and bran

Dairy

- Replace sugary dairy snacks with low-fat yoghurt scooped into a small container – no need to buy individual serves
- Replace processed cheese sticks and slices with pieces of low-fat cheese cut into sticks, e.g. edam, fetta

Meat

- Replace processed luncheon meats with slices of cold meats, e.g. ham, chicken, tuna
- Replace tinned fish in oil with tinned fish in water
- Replace meat with an egg, whole-boiled or in a sandwich

Vegetables

- Replace potato chips with fresh sprouts, pieces of carrot, cherry tomatoes, celery or cucumber and a small container of low-fat dip
- Replace processed salads with fresh salads and sprouts

Drinks

- Replace fruit juice, soft drinks, cordial and flavoured milk with water.

8.

Miracle Skywalker Part 2: Good intentions

I'm in the spare room looking at a big brown box sitting in the middle of the carpet. It looks like a coffin. But it's not. It's the Miracle Skywalker.

It arrived last week, but Dad still hasn't put it together. He hasn't even opened the box.

I go into the lounge room.

He's sitting in his chair drinking a glass of wine and watching the news.

'When are you going to set up the Skywalker, Dad?' I say.

'Soon,' he says, without looking away from the TV.

'Tonight?' I say.

'Not tonight,' he says, watching the news. 'I'm busy.'

'That's what you said last night,' I say.

'That's because I was busy,' he says.

'And the night before that,' I say.

'Look,' says Dad. 'I'll set it up, all right? But just not right now. I've had a long day and I just want to relax.'

'I thought you said you were busy,' I say.

'I *am*!' says Dad. 'Busy relaxing! Go and ask your mother.'

I go into the kitchen.

Mum is stirring a pot full of some weird stuff. It smells like seaweed. I'm not brave enough to ask what it is.

'Mum?' I say. 'Can you put the Skywalker together?'

'Not now, Jack,' she says. 'I'm cooking dinner. Why don't you ask your father? It was his idea.'

'He said he's busy,' I say.

Mum shrugs. 'If you want some exercise, why don't you take Rusty for a walk?'

'That's not exercise,' I say. 'That's just picking up poo. That's poo-ercise!'

'Well, I don't know how to help you then, Jack,' says Mum. 'Why don't you have a go at doing it yourself?'

'I will then!' I say, stomping out of the kitchen.

I tear open the top of the box. There are more plastic bags than I've ever seen in my life. I start pulling them out.

Bags of screws. Bags of nuts. A bag of long shiny silver bits of metal. Bags full of unidentified black plastic shapes. Brackets. Wires. Cords. Handles. Foot straps. Dials. LED display panels.

I pick up the manual.

It's the thickness of a small paperback book.

I open it.

It's full of black-and-white diagrams with tiny black writing underneath.

Hmmm.

I had no idea there was so much to a Miracle Skywalker.

In fact it would be a miracle if I – or anybody for that matter – could actually put it all together.

Besides, I think I've got homework to do.

Maybe the issue is not about carbohydrate and protein ratios or some new super weight loss product. Perhaps it is about us as individuals; how we see our bodies, how we think about food and exercise and how we psychologically approach the process of getting in shape.

– *Craig Harper,* Your Perfect Body

Good intentions are no use if you don't act on them. The most amazing machine is no use unless it's part of a consistent exercise program. Whether you have a machine or not, what is really required is a shift in the way you think about exercise. If you believe that it is one more unpleasant duty to fit into a life already crammed with unpleasant duties it will remain something that somehow you never seem to get around to. If, however, you think of exercise as an activity that unlocks hidden reserves of energy, vitality and wellbeing that will enhance every other area of your life, it is far more likely that you will make the effort to fit it in. Along with the enjoyment and satisfaction to be gained from the exercise itself, you'll soon be wondering how you ever did without it.

Action 3.8
Maintaining motivation to exercise

- Exercise is an excellent mood enhancer. Regular exercise releases endorphins, hormones produced by the body, which give a natural high that can last most of the day.
- A useful technique for making exercise a regular part of your life is to schedule a session in your diary like you would schedule any other appointment. Early in the morning is an excellent time if you can organise it. The session is less likely to get knocked out by other urgent business, and you'll feel the effects for the rest of the day.
- Make a regular weekly appointment with a friend to go for a walk or run. Having someone relying on you means you will be less likely to cancel.

- Invest in a really good pair of walking shoes or runners. Not only will the shoes protect your feet and legs from injury, but purchasing them will be an important step in changing your self-image from a non-exerciser to someone who exercises.
- A radio, tape, CD or MP3 player can be a great addition to your session. Listen to music that motivates you, an audio book, or a relaxation tape. Think of your daily exercise session as time out from other people's demands on you and as an opportunity to replenish yourself, both physically and mentally.

9. Exercise video: Get moving

It's two weeks later. The Miracle Skywalker is still sitting in the spare room. Unassembled.

I'm in the kitchen spooning honey onto a piece of banana cake when Mum comes home.

'Hi, Jack,' she says. 'Come into the living room. I've got something for you.'

I walk into the room.

Mum is pushing all the furniture in the living room to the corners. 'What's going on, Mum?' I say.

'We're going to do some exercise.'

'What?' I say. 'In here?'

'Yes,' says Mum. 'I bought an exercise video. They were recommended in my book.'

'I don't know, Mum,' I say.

Don't be like that,' she says. 'I asked you to walk the dog and you refused. If you don't want to walk then you can at least do the video.'

She presses 'play'.

I stare at the screen as a woman in an orange leotard begins doing star jumps and urging us to do the same.

'Well, come on,' says Mum, already copying her.

'I'm not doing that,' I say.

'Why not?' says Mum. 'It will be good for you.'

'I've got homework,' I say, heading for the door. This is too embarrassing for words.

'Jack,' says Mum sternly. I know better than to ignore this tone in her voice.

'If you do the whole video you can have an ice-cream when you finish.'

Hmmm. I don't like exercise, but I *do* like ice-cream.

I look at the orange leotard lady. She's still doing star jumps.

'Come on, Jack!' says Mum, doing star jumps as well.

I begin doing some half-hearted star jumps. After four I stop. 'There . . . are you happy?'

'That's great, Jack,' says Mum. 'Keep going!'

After about three thousand years the leotard lady stops doing star jumps and tells us to reach for the roof.

I reach for the roof.

Then she tells me to reach for my toes.

I reach for my toes.

I can't get anywhere near them but she says that's okay, just to do what I can.

I put my hands on my hips and lean to the left.

I lean to the right.

I lean to the left again, but I lean a little too far, stagger sideways and crash into the bookshelf. It slams against the wall. I fall flat on my back. Books rain down on my head, including Mum's copy of *Fast Track Your Fitness.*

'Are you okay, Jack?' says Mum, helping me up.

'I think so,' I say. 'Can I have my ice-cream now?'

Given the opportunity children will play 'spontaneously'. In other words, they provide their own motivation to play and act without prompting or intervention by an adult. The type and duration of the play in which they engage is entirely determined by them and activities can be taken up and stopped at will. To the child, playing is an end in itself and to an observer there may not seem to be any obvious goal or conclusion.

– *Mary Sheridan et al,* Play in Early Childhood

Children do not exercise – they play. They do not play for future gains or because it is good for them. They play because it is fun. An extended video workout, no matter how well planned, will be of limited use to children, who tend more naturally to exercise in short bursts. By playing, children practise controlling their movements. They develop gross motor skills such as running, jumping, throwing and catching, as well as fine motor skills such as manipulating small objects. Play is also important in developing vision, providing opportunities for children to focus on objects which are at varying distances. There are many types of play:

- Active play: gaining strength, agility and coordination, e.g. running, jumping, kicking, catching
- Imitative: learning by copying and repetition – helps them to make sense of the world
- Building: manipulating objects to build something – involves planning and insight
- Pretend play: inventing make-believe situations – great for developing imagination
- Games with rules: learning about sharing, taking turns, being in a group.

Action 3.9
Creating a supportive environment for play

To foster play you need:

- A space that lends itself to exploration.
- To turn off the screen. Television shows and DVDs represent other people's ideas and computers use other

people's programs. Children have plenty of their own original thoughts and ideas, but they won't necessarily use them if they don't have to.

- Resources. Children can create their own toys and games with simple equipment such as wooden sticks, cans, plastic containers, glue, scissors, scraps of material, etc.
- Enough time to play without interruption. Guard against overscheduling your child's life with after-school classes and clubs. Adult rules and adult structured environments can be too structured to allow truly child-centred play.
- Friends. A playmate of similar age to play with can be great fun.
- A relaxed attitude. Don't be worried about the 'outcome' of play. Remember, there is no concrete 'product' at the end of playing. The 'doing' is the important thing. Don't try to guide your child to play the way you think they should play, or to construct a particular thing. Offer help if they request it, but let them direct the activity however they please.

10.

The miracle diet: Measle soup with mould

'What's for dinner, Mum?' I say.

'Miso soup,' she says. 'With tofu.'

'Measle soup?' I say. 'With what?'

'Miso,' says Mum. 'It's Japanese. And tofu is made from bean curd. It's an alternative to meat-based protein. It's part of the five-day *Fast Track Your Fitness* cleansing diet.'

'Five days!?' I say. I go over to the stove. It looks like a saucepan full of bubbling mud with little white chunks of mould in it. But I don't say that. She might take it the wrong way.

'Want to try some?' she says.

'Ah, no,' I say. 'Can I have tomato soup instead? Out of a tin?'

'No,' says Mum. 'This is much better for you.

No artificial colourings, flavourings or preservatives for a start. And no sugar. And no fat.'

'But I *like* artificial colouring, flavouring and preservatives,' I say. 'I *like* sugar. I *like* fat. And *I like tomato soup*!'

'Well, you can't have it,' says Mum.

'Well, you can't make me eat *that*,' I say.

'No, I can't,' says Mum. 'But if you don't eat this you're going to be very hungry. And don't think you can just go to your room and eat biscuits. I cleaned out your bedroom today and I got rid of your whole stash.'

Darn. She must have found my food box. But I'm not too worried. I bet she didn't find the Delights hidden under my bed.

'Including the packet of Delights I found hidden under your bed,' continues Mum, as if reading my mind. 'So it's miso soup or nothing.'

'Measle soup?' says Dad, coming into the room.

'MISO soup!' yells Mum.

Dad peers into the saucepan. 'It looks like mud!' he says.

Mum throws the measuring cup at Dad's head. 'Then don't eat it!' she says.

Dad ducks. The cup bounces harmlessly off the wall.

'I didn't mean that in a bad way,' he says. 'I *like* mud.'

Mum looks at him through narrowed eyes.

'What's the white stuff?' says Dad.

'Tofu,' says Mum wearily.

'Mmmm,' says Dad, rubbing his tummy and cocking an eyebrow at me. 'Delicious.'

Mum takes the saucepan off the stove and pours the soup into three bowls. She slides one across the bench to me and pushes one at Dad. 'There you are. Dinner is served.'

'Thanks,' I say. 'Is there any bread to have with it?'

'No,' says Mum.

'Soup without bread?' says Dad. 'Who ever heard of . . .'

'You don't need the extra carbohydrates,' says Mum. 'Especially not at this time of night. Eating too much in the evening is a major cause of weight gain. You've got no chance of burning it off.'

'So what do we have with it?' I say.

Mum pulls a bowl of something out of the refrigerator. It looks like seaweed. But I don't tell her it looks like seaweed. She might take it the wrong way.

'That looks like seaweed,' says Dad.

I flinch.

That was dumb. Very dumb.

But to my utter surprise, Mum just smiles. 'That's because it *is* seaweed,' she says. 'Seaweed salad with sesame seeds. Very high in phyto-nutrients.'

Great. Mud soup with white mould and a side serve of seaweed.

And I thought spinach was bad.

Sometimes we need to forget the high protein, low carbohydrate, low glycemic-index, good fats, bad fats, blah, blah, blah diet debate and just eat less. You do need some fat, protein, carbohydrates, vitamins and minerals but the average Australian diet more than covers those needs, so don't get too paranoid or concerned. The chances of you getting sick from over-indulging and being obese are significantly higher than they are of you getting sick from under-eating or being malnourished. So, put away your diet books and just eat less.

– *Craig Harper,* Your Perfect Body

Most fad diets are too restrictive to maintain over the long term. At their best they may temporarily restrict your intake of calorie-dense foods, causing a short-term weight loss. At their worst, however, the sudden calorie restriction can cause your body's metabolism to slow down, so that you'll have less energy and less fat-burning potential. Then, when you go off the diet, as you inevitably will, you will put on more weight and at the same time find it harder to burn it off than before. It's not easy to suddenly change your – and your family's – eating habits. Do it gradually. The most sensible thing to do is to completely avoid fad diets and make small changes that can be sustained over the long term.

Action 3.10
Some strategies for 'cleaning up' your diet without resorting to fad diets

- Have fresh fruit and vegetables on hand. Find a good supplier and plan to shop there at least once – preferably twice – a week so that your kitchen is always well stocked with fresh, attractive produce. Create a regular standing order with one of the many fruit and vegetable suppliers operating on the internet.
- Eat small, frequent meals. Rather than eating three large meals a day, try cutting down the amount you eat at the main meals and having a mid-morning snack and a mid-afternoon snack. You'll keep your body well supplied with energy all day, and be much less likely to suffer the feeling of raging hunger which often leads to eating more than you really need.
- Control portion sizes. Most people eat too much. They take in more energy than they need. The excess is stored as fat. Try eating the same foods that you always do, but just eat 20 per cent less. Slow down when you eat and really taste your food.

- Cut down on unhealthy fats. Fat is the most concentrated form of energy available to our bodies. There are two main types of fat. Unhealthy fats – those that are solid at room temperature – are saturated fats, mainly animal fats. Many processed foods have added saturated fats, e.g. sweet biscuits, cakes, fried foods. Healthy fats are unsaturated – liquid at room temperature – and are mainly derived from plant foods and non-farmed fish, e.g. olive oil, the oil in avocado and nuts, sesame oil, salmon, tuna.
- Avoid added sugar. Most of us eat way too much of it. Sugar, like fat, is another concentrated form of energy. It contains few nutrients, ruins appetite and has a range of undesirable side effects. Sugar is added to many breakfast cereals, sweet biscuits, soft drinks and juices. Aim for a diet that is 80 per cent composed of foods in their natural state – or as close to it as possible. As foods become more and more refined they become less and less nutritious.
- Drink between six and eight glasses of water every day. Most people do not take enough care to make sure their bodies are properly hydrated. It will not only help you to feel fuller while eating less, but will make you feel better by assisting nutrient flow, muscle growth, brain function and helping to flush toxins from your body.

11.

Swimming centre: You can lead a horse to water, but you can't make it swim twenty laps

I'm naked.

Well, practically naked, except for a pair of too-tight Speedos and a pair of fogged-up goggles.

I'm cold.

And exhausted.

I'm in the middle of the pool, trying desperately to keep my head above the surface.

But it's hard work. I'm sinking fast and all I have to help me are two very tired arms and two 3-tonne legs.

Mum is standing at the side of the pool. 'Keep going, Jack,' she says.

'I can't,' I say.

'You can,' says Mum. 'You're doing well.'

But we both know I'm not. I was supposed to do twenty laps. I'm only halfway through my second. It's about this time that I would normally pinch myself and wake up, but I can't.

This is actually happening.

Mum has brought us all to the pool in a desperate attempt to get us to exercise. Either that or to drown us.

I'm gasping for breath. I accidentally swallow a mouthful of water which triggers a coughing fit.

I've got to get out of here.

I lift my heavy arms and paw at the water like a dog. Somehow, amazingly, I begin to move again.

Flailing and spluttering all the way, I head across the lanes and finally clutch the side of the pool.

Mum crouches down and helps me out.

I sit on the edge, panting and coughing. In the other lanes human torpedoes are churning the water in their wake as they effortlessly chalk up lap after lap.

'How do you feel?' says Mum, draping my towel over my shoulders.

'Terrible,' I say. 'And cold.'

'Okay,' says Mum. 'Have a rest now. You can do the other laps later.'

I nod and retreat to the safety of the benches.

Mum dives in. She's not exactly a human torpedo, but she's doing better than me.

I start to warm up, and as I do, I feel a yawning emptiness in my stomach.

I can see the kiosk from here. Some kids are playing on a video machine.

I pull my T-shirt on, leave Mum to her laps and go over to watch them.

Cool. It's a car-racing game. Something I *am* good at.

'Reckon you've got what it takes to beat a pro?' says a voice behind me. I turn around. A guy with a big wobbly belly is standing behind me. Hang on, I know that man. It's Dad! I realise I haven't seen him in bathers for a long time.

'Course I have,' I say.

Dad puts two one-dollar coins on the machine.

'We'll see about that,' he says.

It doesn't matter what kind of exercise you choose, as long as it fits your lifestyle and you enjoy it enough to continue over time. Swim, walk, run, ride a bike, do aerobics. Variety will stop the boredom and let you enjoy it. To change your metabolic rate, you should exercise four to five times a week; do it

with a fair amount of energy and gusto, and spend a minimum of 30 minutes each day on your exercise session.

– *Cyndi O'Meara,* Changing Habits Changing Lives

It is important to find the exercise that's right for you. If you don't like swimming pools or gymnasiums then don't go to them! There are plenty of other beneficial ways to move your body. It's all about moving and no one way of moving is superior to another. Walking is one of the easiest and most convenient ways of working half an hour of movement into your day. But even that doesn't suit everybody. You might prefer team sports. Or bike-riding. The crucial thing is to find something that you can fit comfortably into your life and that you like doing . . . that doesn't mean it's always going to be easy, but it will mean that there's a high degree of intrinsic motivation to continue the activity.

Action 3.11
Identifying an activity that's right for you

- Make a list of activities that you have enjoyed in the past. Particularly think about what you enjoyed as a child – even if you haven't done the activity since you were twelve years old, this can be a powerful clue as to what activity might suit you now. Just because you haven't done it for a long time doesn't mean you can't start again.

- Do some research. Local papers, local councils, the internet, magazines, books, libraries and specialist shops are all valuable sources of information for finding out about equipment and opportunities in your area. See the Sources and resources section on page 289.
- Be aware that if you embrace an activity with enthusiasm, you will be setting a powerful example for your children. They may not necessarily embrace the activity for themselves, but they will be seeing movement and exercise as a normal and enjoyable part of life.
- Go through the above process with your child. Be aware that there may be a few false starts before they find the activity that's right for them.
- Don't expect that just because you enjoyed an activity as a child that your child should or will enjoy the same activity. Everybody is different.
- If all else fails, at least start walking in the meantime. See Action 4.4, 'Benefits of walking' on page 183.

12.

Phase two: Getting real

Half an hour later Dad and I are still hunched over the machine.

It's two-all.

I'm biting into a hot dog and about to put the coins into the machine for the decider when I feel a tap on my shoulder. 'There you are!' says a voice. 'I've been looking for you.'

It gives me such a start that I knock my cup of Zap! all over the top of the screen. It goes everywhere, pouring over the edges.

Dad jumps up, dropping his pie.

I turn around.

Mum is standing there with her arms folded.

Sprung!

'Have you had a good swim?' she says in a calm

voice. A little too calm, under the circumstances.

Dad and I look at each other.

We look back at Mum.

I can feel Zap! dripping down the back of my leg. The hot dog is going cold in my hand. I really want to take a bite, but I don't dare.

She nods. 'Okay then. Well, I'm so glad we made the effort to come here today. It's great to see you both taking your health seriously.'

The Zap! drips.

'I had a spa,' says Dad meekly. 'It was very invigorating.'

'Great!' says Mum. 'That must have got your heart really pumping. Gee, with that and Jack's lap and a half I'd say you'll both be ready for phase two of the program.'

'Phase two?' says Dad, with a scared look. 'What's phase two?'

'I give up,' says Mum.

'Give up?' says Dad. 'But you *can't*!'

'Why not?' says Mum. '*You* have! I'm the only one trying here. If you don't want to make an effort, fine. I'm not going to make it for you. I *can't* make it for you.'

'I have been trying,' says Dad.

'How, exactly?' says Mum. 'You won't walk. You won't swim. You won't even put the Miracle Skywalker together.'

'I haven't exactly had much time,' says Dad.

'You haven't *made* the time,' says Mum. 'It's obviously just not important enough to you. It doesn't take any time to support me in improving the family's diet, but you just sit there and treat it all like a big joke. Well, laugh it up, funny boy. It's your funeral. And Jack's, too, if you don't start setting a better example.'

She looks intently at each of us and then turns on her heel and stalks off.

'Hey,' yells Dad, across the kiosk. 'Don't be like this.'

Mum turns, shakes her head and then strides off in the direction of the showers.

The Zap! drips.

The hot dog sags.

I don't really feel hungry anymore. I start wiping up the Zap! with a serviette.

'I might just go and do a couple of laps before we go,' says Dad.

'Me too,' I say.

'Race you,' he says.

I chuck the hot dog and soggy serviettes in the bin and run after him.

A lean body never happens by accident. An overweight body never happens by accident. The cause of body fat in most cases is inactivity, poor nutrition and often a negative self-image. Depending on your genetics, you may never look like Mr or Miss Olympia, but you always have the power to improve your body and your health above and beyond where you are today. How? By accepting 100 per cent total responsibility for your situation and then taking positive action every day for the rest of your life to improve it.

– *Tom Venuto,* Big Fat Lies!

The first step to making improvements to your – and your family's – health is cultivating a healthy attitude. How you think has a powerful effect on how you act.

Action 3.12
Cultivating a healthy attitude

- Replace negative thoughts with positive thoughts. Negative beliefs like 'I'm too old to exercise', 'I hate exercise', and 'It's too late to exercise' will become self-fulfilling prophecies and won't benefit you in any way. Every time you catch yourself thinking a negative thought, identify it as such, and then replace it with a positive one like 'I'm getting fitter, stronger and healthier as I age'. If you do this often enough, you'll find your behaviour changes accordingly.

- Introduce changes to your lifestyle gradually. Don't try to do everything at once. Make a small sustainable change, and when that change has become permanent, make another small sustainable change. Go easy on yourself.
- Be patient. It takes 30 to 60 days to change a habit and another 30 to 60 days to make a lifestyle change permanent.
- Avoid 'all or nothing' thinking. One of the biggest barriers to establishing a regular program of movement and healthy eating is the belief that you should either do it every single day or not at all. This belief sets people up for failure. Don't beat yourself up because you missed a few days or a week. Remember that you're in this for the long haul. Better to congratulate yourself for what you've achieved so far, put your running shoes on and get back out there.
- Optimum health is the result of consistently healthy choices, not a 'get fit' binge once or twice a year. It is very unrealistic to expect that you will reach a certain level of fitness and then never have to train again. Fitness is a process, not an endpoint. Set short-, medium- and long-term goals for your exercise by all means, but remember that you're putting a program of movement in place for the rest of your life.

Part 4

The Program – Phase Two

1.

Walking home: The long march

When we emerge from the change room, Mum is nowhere to be found.

'Where do you think she is?' I say.

Dad checks his mobile. 'She says she'll see us at home,' he says. 'She's taken the car.'

'She's *what*?' I say.

'Taken the car,' repeats Dad, who looks as stunned as I feel.

'But how are we going to get home?' I say.

He shrugs. 'I guess we'll have to walk,' he says.

'Walk?' I say. 'But it's too far! Can't we catch a taxi?'

'No,' says Dad. 'I left most of my money at home. And I've spent the money I brought on the video game.'

I shake my head. 'How could you be so dumb, Dad?'

'I've been working on it all my life, son,' he says, putting his arm around my shoulder. 'Come on, let's hit the road!'

The walk is not as long – or as hard – as I thought. In fact, it's kind of fun. When we get home, Dad heads straight for the spare room. 'I think it might be a good time to put the Skywalker together,' he says.

'Can I help?' I say.

'Of course,' he says, taking the lid off the box and surveying the contents. 'I think I'm going to need it.'

We unpack all the pieces, lay them out all over the carpet and two hours later a true miracle happens: the Skywalker is assembled!

'There,' says Dad, rubbing his hands. 'That wasn't so hard, was it?'

'No,' I say. 'Can I have a go?'

'Of course,' he says.

I climb up onto the stocks. I grab the handles. It immediately lunges forwards and I almost fall off. I manage to hang on as the Skywalker lunges backwards . . . forwards . . . and backwards again. Before I know it I'm skywalking like a pro.

I go forwards.

I go backwards.

I go downhill.

I go uphill.

After five minutes I'm puffing heavily. It's not quite as easy as the guy made it look on the ad. He said the machine did the exercise for you. Maybe we got a lazy one.

I get off and Dad climbs on.

'Well,' he says when he's under way, 'how do I look?'

'Kind of stupid,' I chuckle.

'You know,' he says, puffing and panting, 'to tell you the truth, that's how I feel. But it's sort of fun.'

'Yeah,' I say. 'It beats swimming, any day.'

'And you can watch TV at the same time,' says Dad. 'You've got to love that.'

'Yep,' I say. 'That's pretty cool.'

'Jack?' says Mum.

I turn around. Mum is standing in the doorway watching Dad with a quizzical smile on her lips.

'Yes?' I say.

'Who *is* that hunky guy on the Skywalker?' she says.

An old man was walking along the beach, when he came upon a part of the sand where thousands of

starfish had washed ashore. A little further down the beach he saw a young woman, who was picking up the starfish one at a time and tossing them back into the ocean. 'Oh you silly girl,' he exclaimed. 'You can't possibly save all of these starfish. There're too many.' The woman smiled and said, 'I know. But I can save this one,' and she tossed another into the ocean, 'and this one,' toss, 'and this one . . .'

– *Adapted from Randy Poole, 'The Difference He Made'*

When beginning a program of movement there is often a temptation to do too much too soon. Build up gradually. Huge changes are ineffective and unsustainable over the long term. A small change, however, can have great power if applied consistently. And it all counts! Don't make the mistake of thinking that because you can't do an hour of exercise there's no point doing anything. If you only have fifteen minutes, then do fifteen minutes. Fifteen minutes of fast walking can significantly elevate your heart rate, your breathing and make a big difference to your overall sense of wellbeing. Ten minutes on a bike will have a similar effect, as will skipping continuously for five minutes. And if you do nothing but five minutes of skipping a day, every day for a month? You'll be a lot further down the track towards good health than if you hadn't. Don't wait for the perfect time to start an exercise program . . . it may never come. Start with what time and equipment you have right now and take it from there. It all makes a difference.

Action 4.1
Creating a sustainable exercise program

- Resist 'all or nothing' thinking. Don't say 'I'm going to walk for one hour every single day' and then give up when you inevitably fall back into old patterns – it's more effective and realistic to say 'I'm going to look for opportunities to move as often as possible', or 'I'm going to look for ways to gradually cut down the amount of time I'm not moving'. Give your body – and your mind – time to adjust and time to form new habits and new patterns. Then, when the new pattern becomes established, look for ways to improve on it.
- Attend to variety. The same exercise performed over and over – no matter how exciting at first – will get boring, and may cause wear and tear on particular muscles. It's much better to try to incorporate a variety of different activities in a week, e.g. walking, running, swimming, bike-riding.
- A realistic plan for aerobic exercise over a month might be as follows:
  - *Week 1*: A fifteen-minute workout every second day.
  - *Week 2*: A fifteen-minute workout most days.
  - *Week 3*: A fifteen-minute workout every second day, a half-hour walk every other day.
  - *Week 4*: A half-hour workout every second day, a 45-minute walk every other day.

Increase exercise gradually. Listen to your body. Take notice of how you feel and adjust your activity level accordingly.

2.
Jack's bedroom: The case of the missing TV

It's 4.00 pm. I get home, sling my school bag into my bedroom and stop dead.

Oh no!

There's a gap in my bookshelf where the television used to be!

'Mum!' I yell. 'We've been robbed!'

Mum comes into my room. 'Robbed?' she says.

'Look!' I say, pointing at the empty space. 'My TV's gone!'

'You're right,' says Mum.

'Should we call the police?' I say.

'No,' says Mum.

'Why not?' I say.

'Because *I* took it,' she says.

Her confession takes me by surprise.

'YOU took it?' I say. 'But why . . . hang on . . . I know why . . . because you're going to replace it with a 70-centimetre plasma screen?'

Mum shakes her head. 'No,' she says.

'An 80-centimetre plasma screen?' I say hopefully.

'No,' says Mum.

'One of those overhead projectors with a super-size screen and surround sound?' I say.

'No,' says Mum.

'Then what?' I say.

'Nothing,' she says.

'But what am I supposed to watch?' I say.

'Well,' says Mum, 'your father and I have decided to limit your television viewing to one hour a day, so it shouldn't be a big inconvenience to use the television in the lounge room.'

Barely recovered from the shock of losing my television and the disappointment of not getting a wide screen or an overhead projector with surround sound, I'm sent reeling by this second, even more unexpected blow. 'One hour?' I say. 'ONE hour?'

'Yes,' says Mum. 'We think that's enough.'

'You might think it's enough,' I say. 'But *I* don't!'

'Well, we do,' says Mum. 'You're just going to have to choose which program you want to watch the most.'

'But there are too many!' I say. 'I can't choose just one!'

'Too bad,' says Mum.

'Do you mean just on weekdays?' I say.

'No,' says Mum. 'Weekends as well.'

'But . . . but . . .' I stammer, 'what am I going to *do*?'

'Play,' says Mum simply.

I look at her. Poor Mum. She doesn't understand.

'Play?' I say. 'On the computer?'

'Outside,' says Mum wearily. 'Go to the park. Take the dog for a walk. I don't care. Just don't sit there watching television.'

'So you don't want me to have any friends, is that it?' I say.

'What are you talking about, Jack?' says Mum.

'That's just it,' I say. 'I won't *have* anything to talk about. Everyone will be talking about what happened on *Big Brother* and I won't even know what they're talking about.'

'Well, you could listen to them,' says Mum.

'It's not the same,' I say.

'Well, why don't you make that the program that you watch?' says Mum.

'But then I won't be able to watch *Giant Fighting Robot Man*!' I say. 'Don't you understand anything?'

'As a matter of fact,' says Mum, 'I do. I understand that you're spending too much time watching television and we're doing something about it.'

'*You're* doing something about it,' I say.

'And if your friends won't be friends with you because you don't watch TV then it's probably time for you to get some new friends,' says Mum.

'But EVERYONE watches TV,' I say.

'And so will you,' says Mum. 'One hour a day.'

'You'll never get away with this!' I say.

'Why not?' says Mum.

'Because I'm calling the police.'

'Good for you,' says Mum. 'If they're looking for me, tell them I've gone to the shop to get some milk. You can come too, if you like.'

Mum leaves the room.

I stand there, looking dumbly at the gap in the bookshelf where the TV used to be.

For a fat child . . . turning the television or the computer off may be a more effective technique for weight loss than trying to get that child involved in a sport or other active pastime.

– *Garry Egger,* Trim for Life

Limiting TV viewing is a powerful move. First, it will dramatically decrease your child's exposure to advertisements for fast food. Secondly, it will decrease the amount of time your child spends eating while watching TV. Thirdly, watching TV uses less energy than sleeping or simply sitting there *not* watching TV, so *anything* that your child does will use more energy. Lastly, and perhaps most importantly of all, it increases the opportunity for active play, with the potential for even more energy expenditure and for reducing reliance on the TV for entertainment.

Studies have shown that obesity is lowest among children who watch television for one hour or less a day.

Action 4.2
Guidelines and hints for workable television budgeting

- Reduce your own viewing to one hour a day. Remember the power of being an effective role model.
- Ease into it. The less TV your child watches, the less they will want to watch, as they will not be exposed to so many enticing promos. They will soon find other things to do. Reduce daily viewing time by half an hour a week until they are down to a maximum of one hour a day. Encourage them to record programs and watch them later when they can also fast-forward through the ads.
- Budget computer gaming as well – this activity is equally sedentary. Use a countdown timer (many mobile phones now have these built in).

- An effective method for limiting TV viewing is to work out a system whereby time for watching TV is earned. For instance, one hour of helping around the house = half an hour of TV.
- Be careful not to make other activities appear to be punishment. Instead, explain that there are a lot of fun things besides watching television that you would like them to enjoy.
- See Action 1.1, 'Strategies to limit the influence of TV advertising' on page 6, and Action 4.3, 'Strategies for dealing with active children' on page 178 for more ideas.

3.
The backyard: Go outside and play!

I slide open the back door, blinking against the bright sunshine.

Rusty lifts his head and looks at me as if to say, 'Hey, what are *you* doing out here?!'

I pat his head and sit down on the back step with him. I'm not exactly sure what the answer to Rusty's question is.

But Rusty is in no doubt at all.

He gets up, retrieves a bald tennis ball from the grass and drops it at my feet. He steps back, looking expectantly at the ball.

'You really want it?' I say, picking it up. 'Go get it!' I throw it to the back of the yard.

Rusty takes off. He lunges for it at such speed that he crashes into the back fence. Then he drops it back at my feet. It's not exactly PlayStation, but it's kind of fun.

We repeat this over and over until the ball is drenched in dog spit. Rusty's back legs are shaking and he's panting so hard he looks like he's about to have a heart attack.

If this was PlayStation and he really *did* have a heart attack I'd just call up a new dog, but this is real. And I don't think killing the dog was exactly what Mum had in mind when she said, 'Go outside and play.'

'Take a break, mate,' I say, filling his water bowl. He sticks his nose in and laps up huge mouthfuls.

While he's doing this I notice a trail of ants leading from his bowl. I follow them up the concrete path, across the grass to an anthill underneath the clothesline.

The clothesline!

Why didn't I think of it?!

I wind it up to its full extension, take a run up, jump on and take off.

I lift up my knees and go around a few times.

Rusty starts chasing me, snapping at my feet.

Now this *is* fun.

I'm swinging at about a thousand kilometres an hour when the clothesline groans and lurches. My knees hit the ground.

I let go of the line and fall onto my back. I'm looking up at the clouds, puffing.

Puffing and laughing.

I haven't done that for ages.

I sit up.

Uh-oh.

Doesn't look like I'll be doing it again for ages, either.

The clothesline is leaning at a 45-degree angle to the ground.

I stand up, jump onto the high end and try to bend it back the way it was. But it only seems to make it worse.

'Jack!' yells Mum. 'What do you think you're doing?'

'I'm trying to fix the clothesline,' I say.

'But it wasn't broken,' she says.

'I know,' I say, 'but it is now.'

'Because you were swinging on it!' she says.

'It was your idea,' I say.

'I told you to go outside and play,' she says. 'Not go outside and destroy the clothesline.'

'Well, you should have *said* that,' I say.

'Why you cheeky . . .' she says, coming down the back steps towards me with her hands outstretched.

I run. She chases me.

Now *this* is what I call fun.

I think I'm going to come outside and play more often.

Opportunities for incidental physical activity (physical activity which occurs as part of lifestyle routines, such as walking to work, buying milk from the corner store, cycling to a friend's place) are shrinking and being replaced by technology; modern transport systems; increased safety concerns and a reduction in local neighbourhood opportunities e.g. safe neighbourhood parks and places. We have 'taken kids off the streets' for their own protection and our social safety, but maybe we need to put them back! Children no longer walk to school; play in the street; climb – and fall out of trees; or use public transport. Is it surprising to see that obesity rates in children are increasing significantly?

– *Gary Henshall,* Encouraging Participation in Active Leisure

Screen entertainment such as TV, CDs, DVDs and computer games are fun for most children. There is no reason why they shouldn't be able to be entertained in this way some of the time. The issue becomes one of balance. A child in front of a screen seems happy, quiet, non-argumentative, not making a mess and not in any physical danger. Having too much time in front of a screen, however, can create a passive, inactive child. If a child feels they have nothing else to do, or has nothing they are interested in doing, they are probably spending too much time in front of the screen. Children are, by nature, curious and active beings. As parents, it is our responsibility to provide them with alternatives to screen games. The benefits to our children's health – both in the short and long term – will more than outweigh the inconvenience.

Action 4.3
Strategies for dealing with active children

- Be positive. Don't give in after a few minutes of 'I'm bored'. Break the boredom barrier (it usually takes ten to fifteen minutes): remember, children are hard-wired to play. TVs are a relatively recent arrival in the lives of young – and older – human beings.
- Be aware of not sending mixed messages to your child when they go outside, for instance, 'Don't get dirty', or 'Be careful', or 'Don't break anything!' You may inadvertently be conveying a negative message about active play which leads to their being more reluctant to go outside next time.
- Kids will play spontaneously, but they need unstructured free time to do so. Try not to get too busy and overcomplicate or overcrowd days.
- Children may initially need your time and support in getting started on an activity, but don't feel that you have

to play with them the whole time. Learning to be independent is part of playing.

- Make sure equipment and encouragement are provided for TV/computer game alternatives. See Action 4.11, 'Alternatives to "conventional" exercise' on page 221 and Action 5.7, 'Simple resources for encouraging inside play' on page 268 for ideas.
- Make a point of discovering what your local parks have to offer. Many suburbs now have impressive adventure playgrounds. See Action 4.12, 'Active family outings' on page 226 for more ideas.

4. Pedometer challenge: Part 1

I wake up. There is a nice smell coming from the kitchen.

I get out of bed and go in.

'Good morning,' says Mum, putting a steaming bowl onto the table in front of me. 'There's your porridge. And here's your toy.' She puts a small box next to the bowl.

'Thanks,' I say. 'What is it?'

'A pedometer,' says Mum.

'Cool!' I say. 'I've seen these on TV!'

'Morning,' says Dad, hobbling into the kitchen. 'I think I might have overdone it a bit on the Skywalker yesterday.'

'Me too,' I say. 'My arms are really sore.'

'My whole body is really sore,' says Dad.

'Gee,' says Mum, 'if you feel this bad, imagine

how the Skywalker must feel, considering it's supposed to be doing all the work.'

But Dad's not listening. He's more interested in my new toy. 'What's that?' he says.

'A pedometer,' I say.

Dad peers at it. 'Okay,' he says, 'but *what* is it?'

'It's a counter,' I say, clipping it onto my pants. I start pacing up and down the kitchen, counting aloud: 'One, two, three . . .'

'And the point is . . . ?' says Dad.

'It keeps track of how many steps you take in a day,' says Mum, putting one in Dad's hand. 'I got you one too. You're supposed to take 10,000 steps a day.'

'What?' says Dad. 'Who's got that sort of time?'

'It says here that it only takes between 30 and 45 minutes a day,' says Mum, reading from the instructions.

'And we can have competitions!' I say. 'Come on, Dad. Put it on. Last to 100 is a rotten egg.'

'Hang on,' he says, fumbling with the clip. 'Like that?'

Mum adjusts it and pushes the start button. Dad takes a few slow exaggerated steps like he's walking on the moon. 'That's one small step for man . . .' he jokes. 'One giant leap for . . .'

'Come on, Dad,' I say, striding off down the hallway.

'You didn't say "Go!"' says Dad, chasing after me.

Mum follows.

Half an hour, twenty competitions and 2000 steps each later, we're sitting – red-faced and panting – in the kitchen.

'Can we do this again tonight?' I say.

Mum smiles. 'Sure,' she says. 'If you can handle it.'

'What do you mean?' I say.

'Your mission – should you choose to accept it – is to get your pedometer to 8000 steps by six o'clock.'

'Tonight?' I say.

'Tonight,' says Mum.

'What do I get if I do it?' I say.

'The satisfaction of knowing that you did it,' says Mum.

'Is that all?' I say.

'And dessert,' says Mum.

I nod. This just got serious.

Above all, do not lose your desire to walk: every day I walk myself into a state of wellbeing and walk away from every illness; I have walked myself into my best thoughts, and I know of no thought so burdensome that one cannot walk away from it . . . the more one

sits still, the closer one comes to feeling ill . . . Thus if one just keeps on walking, everything will be all right.

– *Søren Kierkegaard, letter to* Jette, *1847*

A pedometer is an excellent way of seeing just how much – or how little – exercise you've done in a day. Unlike the Miracle Skywalker or the measle soup with mould cleansing diet, it does not promise results without effort – it is simply a tool that helps you to monitor your progress. Most adults take an average of 6000 to 7000 steps a day. To maintain a basic level of fitness, however, research indicates a recommended daily step count of no fewer than 10,000 steps. Fewer than 5000 steps a day is simply not enough and is considered sedentary. An adult who takes 12,500 steps a day is highly active. For a child to maintain a basic level of fitness they need to take around 15,000 steps a day at least five days a week. Although this seems many more than for an adult, children's steps are generally smaller and quicker, and reaching 15,000 steps in a day is no more difficult to achieve than for an adult to reach 10,000.

Action 4.4
Benefits of walking

- Simple. There are no new skills to learn, and it can be done anywhere, anytime.
- Body maintenance. Walking helps to restore joint mobility, improves lung capacity and function, reduces high blood pressure, improves digestion, improves posture.

- Invigorating. Walking leaves you feeling calm, alert and refreshed.
- Slimming. Practised on a daily basis, combined with sensible eating, walking helps to reduce excess stores of fat.
- Variable. You can continually adjust the intensity level depending on your level of fitness. Walking faster and/or uphill will make the activity more intense and deliver even greater benefits. You can also change the locations to avoid boredom.
- See Action 1.3, 'Easy ways to increase the amount of movement in your day' on page 16.

5.

Pedometer challenge: Part 2

'Mum, can you drop me here?' I say.

'Here?' says Mum. 'But we're still two blocks away, at least!'

'I know,' I say. 'But I want to get my count up. And I'll walk home tonight.'

'Of course,' says Mum, pulling over. 'Just be careful, and don't forget to . . .'

'I know,' I say. 'Cross at the lights. You've only told me about forty thousand times.'

Mum smiles. 'Sorry,' she says. 'Have a good day. And good luck!'

I get out, start walking and, incredibly, make it to school without being run over.

I check my pedometer.

Three thousand, three hundred.

I need more.

I walk around the school a couple of times to bring it up to 4000.

Jeremy's going to have to play golf without me. I've got my pride to worry about. Not to mention dessert.

At lunchtime I go to the canteen the long way, via the playground.

It adds 200 steps.

I go the long way back to the library.

It adds 300 steps.

Good, but not enough.

I need another 1000 at least if I'm going to have any chance of making the 8000 by 6.00 pm. And I'm not going into the library until I've got them.

It takes me four times around the school.

I go into the library and play one game before the bell rings.

That afternoon I walk home from school. I refuse to let myself check the pedometer until I'm inside.

I flop down into my favourite TV chair.

My feet are sore.

I reckon I've walked more today than I have in my whole life. I've probably pushed the pedometer to breaking point. Eight thousand? Try 80,000!

I remove it from my belt and open it.

Huh?

This can't be right.

Six thousand, three hundred!

This is terrible!

I've walked and I've walked and I've walked and I'm still 1700 steps short! And it's 4.30!

Dad will be home in one hour. He probably hasn't completed his 8000, either.

But what if he has?

He's not going to beat me.

I have to get my steps up.

But how?

I hear Rusty pawing at the back door.

I know what I must do. Desperate times call for desperate measures.

'Mum?' I call. 'Where's Rusty's leash?'

Recent research suggests that an activity does not have to be continuous for weight loss. Accumulated activity may be as effective as continuous activity, hence the new physical activity guideline to accumulate, or put together, 30 minutes of moderate-intensity activity per day.

– National Health and Medical Research Council, 'Clinical practice guidelines for the Management of Overweight and Obesity in Adults'

You don't have to get all your exercise in one exhausting formal exercise session. You can space it out during the day, or even the week. A bit here and a bit there: it all adds up. The bottom line is that you're aiming for around 30 minutes a day of moderate to vigorous exercise. Now this is only a guideline and not something to get hung up about. It may be easier to think of it spread over a week, say 6 x 30 minutes = 180 minutes or three hours. If you employ a few of the strategies for getting extra exercise in during your days and then go for even just one longer formal exercise session (say a one-hour walk) on the weekend you'll easily make up the time and the daily step count.

Action 4.5
Adapting to exercise

- Although any degree of exercise may be uncomfortable when you start, your body will quickly adapt. Blood supply to your muscles increases, muscle mass increases slightly, fat in the area is burned off and your joints improve their flexibility. This 'adaptation response' of the body is what you experience as fitness and wellbeing. The key to ever-increasing levels of these is to continually make small increases in either the intensity or duration of the exercise. You need to keep giving your body something new and more challenging to adapt to.
- Intensity refers to the amount of effort you are putting into a particular activity. To increase the intensity of an activity like walking, you might try walking uphill, or alternating a

few minutes of fast walking with a few minutes of slow walking. A good guide to exercising at a safe but challenging level of intensity is to exercise at a level where you are lightly puffing, but still able to have a conversation.

- Duration refers to the length of time you perform the activity. Thirty to 45 minutes is usually more than enough for a daily session. If you find that you're not sufficiently challenged by this, it may be a sign that it's time to increase the intensity.
- Don't overdo it! It's much better – and safer – to make small weekly increases in either intensity or duration than to make huge changes before your body is ready to cope with them. Consult your doctor if you're uncertain about what's safe for you. A good rule of thumb is not to increase more than 10 per cent a week.
- The following program is an example of how you might do this.
  - *Week 1*: Start off walking normal pace along the street to one lamppost, then double your speed to the next lamppost. Recover by walking at normal speed to the next lamppost and then double your speed to the next lamppost, and so on.
  - *Week 2*: Do the same but increase duration of exercise by five minutes.
  - *Week 3*: Walk normal pace along the street to one lamppost, and then jog slowly to the next and so on. Cut back duration of session by five minutes less than Week 2.

- *Week 4*: Do the same as Week 3 but increase duration by five minutes.
- *Week 5*: Slow jog along the street to one lamppost, double your speed to the next lamppost and so on. Decrease duration of session by five minutes less than Week 4.
- *Week 6*: Increase duration by five minutes.
- *Week 7*: Jog at a steady pace for two lamppost lengths, double your speed to the next lamppost. Decrease duration by five minutes less than Week 6.
- *Week 8 to Week ?*: Keep making small but steady increases in either duration or intensity each week. Take notice of how you're feeling. Don't push too hard and don't strain.

NB: See the basic circuit training program included in the Sources and resources section on page 298.

6.
Food cupboard: A little spring-clean

When I get home Mum is standing in front of the food cupboard with a black plastic garbage bag. I can see a box of Enduro-crunch, a packet of Koala Bix and a bottle of red cordial poking out of the top of the bag.

'Mum?' I say. 'What are you doing?'

'Just a little spring-clean,' says Mum, dropping a box of Fruties into the bag.

'A *little* spring-clean?' I say. 'It looks like a *big* one to me.'

'Well, it's been a while,' says Mum.

'But what's wrong with all this stuff?' I say. 'Is it stale?'

'No,' says Mum.

'Is it past its use-by date?'

'No,' says Mum.

'Then why?' I say.

'Because we don't need it anymore,' says Mum.

'I do,' I say, reaching into the bag and rescuing the Fruties. 'Can't I keep these?'

'No,' says Mum, taking them out of my hand. 'Have a piece of fruit.' She points to the fruit bowl on the bench.

'But it's a waste!' I say.

'I know,' says Mum. 'I should never have bought them in the first place. Do you realise how little fruit is actually in those things?'

I shrug. I haven't got time for that now. I've got a bigger problem. Mum's got a packet of Tangs in her hand! 'Not my Tangs!' I say.

'I'm afraid so,' says Mum.

'But they're *my* Tangs!' I say.

'Then say goodbye to them,' says Mum.

'Why?' I say.

'Because I think you've eaten quite enough for one lifetime,' says Mum.

'But I'm not dead yet!' I say. 'Besides, a barbecue is not a barbecue without Tangs.'

Mum picks up the Toaster Treats.

'Not the Toaster Treats!' I say.

'Yes, the Toaster Treats,' says Mum. 'Do you realise how much sugar is in these things?'

'I don't care, Mum,' I say. 'Honestly, I don't mind.'

'*I* do,' says Mum.

'But what are we going to eat?' I say.

'Jack,' says Mum, 'it might surprise you to know that people have been known to survive for quite long periods on foods other than Fruties, Toaster Treats and Tangs.'

'I don't want to survive without Fruties, Toaster Treats and Tangs,' I say.

'You won't have to,' says Mum.

'You've changed your mind?' I say, hoping that Mum has realised how crazy she's being.

'No,' says Mum. 'We'll be able to buy them occasionally. We just won't have them in the house all the time.'

'But what if a special occasion happens without warning?' I say. 'What will you do then?'

'I'll send you down to the milk bar to buy some,' says Mum. 'It's not a problem.'

'Not for you,' I say.

'In the meantime,' says Mum, 'there's plenty to eat if you need a snack. Nuts, apples, bananas, carrots, sprouts, hommus, wholemeal bread, honey, homemade muesli, and if you're thirsty, have a glass of water.'

I nod, take an apple from the bowl and leave the kitchen.

It's too painful.

The elimination of foods with chemical additives and the substitution of unprocessed foods with higher nutritive values can have a profoundly beneficial effect on childhood and adolescent behavioural patterns. It also results in significant improvement in scholastic performance.

– *HE Buttram and R Piccola,* Our Toxic World

Healthy eating is not difficult or complicated. And it can be considerably less expensive than eating processed foods. Many people, however, think of packaged food as 'convenient' and foods in their natural state as 'non-convenient'. But is a processed muesli bar really *that* much more 'convenient' than a handful of raw nuts and a fresh apple? The only convenient thing most so-called convenience foods offer over fresh food is that they are a convenient source of saturated fats, sugar, salt and food additives, all of which healthy children – and healthy adults – can well afford to do without.

Historically, food processing was used to preserve fresh food, e.g. drying fruit or making cheese from milk. Food processing has now become a complex science, in which some foods are changed so dramatically that they bear no resemblance to their original state, with many valuable vitamins, minerals and antioxidants being lost in the process.

It may also remove important components of food that even food scientists are unaware of. If you want to make things really simple and do the best thing for your body, avoid foods with labels as much as possible. Gradually make them as small a part of your diet as you can and increase the amount of fresh, unprocessed fruits, vegetables and meats you eat. When you do this you are eating foods the way nature intended. They are high in the nutrients your body needs, and their calorie counts aren't artificially increased by processing. It's a win–win situation.

Action 4.6
Planning for a fresh food home

- Plan ahead. Think about what meals you might like to cook in the coming week and plan your shopping list accordingly. Don't wait until 4.00 pm on the day to decide what you're having for dinner that night . . . this is just a recipe for takeaway.
- Establish a shopping routine for buying fresh fruit and vegetables. It's easier to eat the food you want if you have it on hand. Alternatively, arrange for a standing order from both the supermarket and your local greengrocer to be delivered weekly.
- Buy fruit and vegetables in season. They are not only cheaper, they taste a lot better. And, usually, the fresher and closer a food is to the state it occurs in nature, the more nutrients it is likely to contain.

- Search for and find a butcher who sells good cuts of lean meat.
- Buy treats when you need them. If they aren't in the house, then you are less likely to eat them. Sure, you might pay more for a pack of sweet biscuits at the corner shop, but remember, you'll be saving money by not buying them every week. Plus you'll end up healthier.

7.

To market, to market: Real food

We're at the market.

It's crowded. There are people yelling and the air is full of the smell of donuts and coffee mixed with bananas and hot bread and ripe apples and peanuts and cake and fish.

But best of all, there are long tables full of very cool, very cheap toys.

I love it here!

'Come on, Jack,' says Mum, pulling me away from a table full of battery-operated cars.

'Can I get this, Mum?' I ask, holding up this cool little remote-control buggy.

'No, Jack,' says Mum.

'But it's only ten dollars,' I say.

'No,' says Mum. 'We're not here to buy toys.'

'Then what are we here for?' I say, putting the buggy back down onto the table.

'Food,' says Mum.

'Food?' I say. 'We can get that at the supermarket. But not remote-control buggies. Not for *ten dollars.*'

'But I don't want a remote-control buggy,' says Mum.

'I do,' I say. 'Don't I count?'

'Of course you do,' says Mum. 'That's why we're going to buy some fresh fruit and vegetables.'

'I'd rather a buggy,' I say.

She leads me to long tables full of more fruit and vegetables than I've ever seen in my life. And quite a few that I've never seen in my life. I pick up a spiky red ball. 'What's this?' I ask Mum.

Mum frowns. 'I'm not sure,' she says.

'Lychee!' booms a red-faced man beside us. 'Beautiful!'

'Can we get it?' I say. I figure that even if it doesn't taste good, it will come in handy as a weapon.

Mum hands it to the man.

I pick up a bright-green blob. 'And this?' I say.

'Capsicum,' says Mum. 'Goes well on pizza.'

'Pizza!' I say. 'Let's have pizza for dinner! Oh no . . . I suppose that's not healthy.'

'That all depends on how you make it,' says Mum. 'We can pick up a few wholemeal pita bread bases, some mozzarella, olives, chicken and a couple more vegies and we've got ourselves some healthy pizzas. You can make them if you like.'

I'm not sure I like the sound of the words 'wholemeal' and 'vegies' but it sounds better than no pizza at all. And she didn't say anything about spinach or seaweed.

We buy some mushrooms, cherry tomatoes and onions and then wander down the tables. Mum lets me pick anything I want, and pretty soon we've got a cardboard box full of what even I have to admit is a pretty nice-looking assortment of fruit and vegetables.

'Look at that,' says Mum as she pays. 'All that for less than the price of a dinner at Lotza Pizza!'

'Now can we get that buggy?' I say.

'No!' says Mum. 'Have a banana instead.'

Poor Mum. She just doesn't get it.

Who ever heard of a remote-control banana?

I believe that the way to introduce children to great-tasting food that just happens to be good for them is to engage their curiosity, and let them enjoy the widest possible range of flavours and textures in a supportive environment.

– Stephanie Alexander, Age, 13 July 2004

Not only does fresh food have the vitamins, minerals and antioxidants that are often lost in processing, it is cheaper as well. Ask any savvy homemaker on a budget and they can tell you that buying fresh food in season is the cheapest way to feed a family. Processing food costs money and that cost is passed on to the consumer, e.g. potato chips cost around ten times more than the cost of the potatoes used to make them. A 3-kilogram bag of fresh apples in season is the same price as a 125-gram packet of eight fruit roll ups. If you were to buy a litre of pure fruit juice at the same price as you pay for it in a 5 per cent juice fruit drink you would pay $40 per litre.

Action 4.7
Fresh versus processed

- Although markets can initially be daunting, by shopping there regularly you will quickly work out which stores offer both quality produce and value. If you know what you're looking for it's usually possible to pick up great bargains at the end of the day.
- Make it fun. A busy market is a wonderful sensory experience for children – give them time to explore the areas they would like to see.
- Food should not be treated like a medical prescription. Eat for the pleasure and variety of it. Aim to consume a wide variety of different fruits and vegetables each day.

- Children learn by helping. Fresh food is delicious and they will learn this if they help to choose, cook and prepare it.
- Grow a few simple things in your backyard or in pots, e.g. lettuce, basil and cherry tomatoes.

8. Jack's kitchen: Setting the table

I'm standing at the kitchen bench slicing mushrooms for the pizza with the sharp knife. Mum's never let me use the sharp knife before.

I feel like a famous TV chef.

'What I'm doing now is slicing the mushrooms,' I explain to the invisible camera. 'Chop them up really small, but kids, if you're using the sharp knife, be careful!'

I wink at my fans and cut the mushrooms into smaller and smaller cubes.

'Then, when you've got them really really small, just sprinkle them over the pizza base, like this.'

I sprinkle the mushrooms over the pizzas. My program is called *Jack's Kitchen* and it's hugely popular. Even with kids. I've got spin-off books,

DVDs and concert tours. I've even got a range of ultra-sharp kitchen knives with my signature on them.

I wave my knife in the air with my trademark flourish and point it at the viewer. 'So,' I say. ' "Is that all there is to it?" I hear you say. Well, no . . . now we've got to cut the capsicum!'

I pull three capsicums from the bag and juggle them. It's small touches like this that keep my viewers so amused. But my juggling skills are not quite as well developed as my cooking skills and the capsicums end up all over the floor.

'Who are you talking to?' says Mum, coming into the room.

'Nobody,' I say, quickly bending down to pick up the capsicums before Mum sees them.

'And what are those capsicums doing all over the floor?' says Mum. 'Have you been juggling again, Jack?'

'No,' I say quickly. 'They fell.'

'All three?'

'Yes,' I say, but I can tell Mum doesn't believe me.

Luckily Dad comes into the room.

'Who's coming for dinner?' says Dad, frowning at the dinner table.

Mum has put out the sailing ship placemats, a single white candle, and she's got music playing.

'No-one,' says Mum.

'But the table's set,' says Dad.

'Yes,' says Mum. 'I thought it might be nice to sit up at the table tonight.'

'But we can't see the TV from the table,' says Dad.

'I thought we could talk,' says Mum.

'Talk?' says Dad. 'What about?'

'I don't know,' says Mum. 'I dare say we'll think of something.'

'But what about the news?' says Dad. 'How are we supposed to keep up with what's happening in the world if we're all just sitting at the table talking?'

'Read the newspaper,' says Mum.

'At the table?' says Dad hopefully.

'Afterwards,' says Mum.

Dad shakes his head, smiling. 'Don't tell me,' he says. 'It's part of the *program*.'

Mum nods and leads him into the living room. 'Come and sit down and tell me all about your day,' she says. 'Jack's cooking tonight.'

Dad flashes a worried glance over his shoulder.

I flourish my knife at him and then turn my attention back to the camera.

'Now I'm going to show you all a fantastic way to cut tomatoes,' I say.

As the training grounds for future generations and important sites of reconnection for current ones, meals should be welcomed as opportunities for interaction rather than chores to be completed as quickly as possible. They should make people want to linger, while enjoying the company, the conversation and the food.

– Gwendolyn Stansbury, 'Arresting Fast Food'

Human beings evolved as food-sharing animals. We have a long history of eating together that is now being challenged. There is a sense of rushing in our lives that causes mealtimes to be of low priority. Not having a meal prepared and family members not being around at mealtimes make sharing meals impossible. There are many benefits of eating together as a family, even if it is only one or two meals a week. Studies have shown that shared mealtimes lead to increased consumption of fruits and vegetables, and reduced consumption of fried food, soft drink and harmful fats. (Home-cooked meals contain, on average, 10 per cent less fat than a restaurant or takeaway meal.) In addition, eating together improves communication and gives family members a sense of connection with each other which provides a positive boost to mental and emotional health as well as the physical benefits.

Action 4.8
Tips for family mealtimes

- If it's not possible to eat together every night of the week, select one night for a family night.
- Involve children in the selection of a meal and get them to help prepare it.
- Turn off the television. Talk to each other instead. Suggest that each family member contribute a story about their day/week. Keep a family book to record them. Update it at these meals.
- Make it special. Use a tablecloth. Light a candle.

9. Slowing down: The art of slow eating

Mum and I are sitting at the dinner table, waiting for Dad to get the pizza out of the oven.

'Aaagh! Ooh! Ouch!' says Dad, dropping the pizza onto a plate in front of us. 'That's hot!'

'Why didn't you use oven mitts?' says Mum.

'Because I didn't know it was that hot!' says Dad, shaking his hands.

I shrug and reach across the table for a slice. Dad might be in pain, but I'm starving.

Mum taps me on the back of the hand. 'Hang on, Jack!' she says.

'What?' I say.

'Not so fast!' says Mum.

'What are we waiting for?' I say.

'Your father to sit down, for one,' says Mum.

'And the salad, for another. Can you go and get it please? I think your father is injured.'

I go into the kitchen and grab the bowl of salad.

'Don't forget the oven mitts,' says Dad.

'I don't need them,' I say. 'It's not hot.'

'That's what I thought about the pizza,' says Dad.

I bring it back to the table and put it down between a bowl of steamed corn cobs and the water jug.

'Well,' says Dad, rubbing his hands. 'This is very fancy! All we need now is a waiter to serve it.'

'We've already got one,' says Mum.

'Who?' says Dad.

'You!' says Mum.

Dad serves us each a slice of pizza. Mum passes me the salad bowl. I pick out a few lettuce leaves, sprouts and pieces of tomato. I pass on the radish.

I start cramming the pizza into my mouth as fast as I can.

'Slow down, Jack,' says Mum. 'It's not a race.'

'I know,' I say, reaching for a second piece, 'but I'm hungry.'

'You didn't even taste that first piece,' says Mum.

'Yes I did,' I say. 'It tasted good!'

'Okay,' says Mum. 'But I want you to smell the next piece before you take a bite.'

'Smell it?' says Dad. 'Why? Is it off?'

'No,' says Mum. 'I just want us all to slow down and really notice what we're eating.'

Dad looks at me and frowns. I look at Dad and shrug back. I bring the pizza up to my nose and take a deep breath in. 'Mmmmmm,' I say.

'Well?' says Mum.

'It's smells like . . .' I say. 'It smells like . . .'

'Like what, Jack?' says Mum.

'Like pizza!' I say.

Dad guffaws. 'Good one, Jack!' he says.

Mum shakes her head. 'Very funny,' she says.

But the really funny thing is that as I continue to hold the pizza in front of my nose, the smell starts to take on a life of its own. I can smell cheese, and tomato, and onion and capsicum, sure, but at the same time they're blended into a smell that's like all of them but none of them. It's really difficult to describe. But it's nice. Mum was right. I didn't really smell the pizza the first time around. In fact I don't know if I've *ever* really smelled a pizza.

Suddenly I feel a sharp burning sensation in my nose.

Ouch! I was concentrating so hard on the smell that I forgot the cheese was still hot. I drop the pizza.

'Jack!' says Mum.

'I burnt my nose,' I say.

Dad laughs. 'That reminds me of the time Jack thought your red wine was cordial. Remember?' he says.

'Oh yeah!' I say. 'I took a big mouthful and spat it out straightaway!'

'All over me!' says Mum, laughing.

I pick up my pizza. 'Mum?' I say.

'It's all right, Jack,' says Mum. 'You don't have to apologise.'

'No, I wasn't going to,' I say.

'What then?' says Mum.

'Um,' I say. 'Can we do this again tomorrow night?'

At the beginning, it might feel silly to look at the food, to smell the food, to chew slowly and put your fork and knife down between bites, but then it becomes habitual. After a while, you can find ecstatic enjoyment in a single piece of fine dark chocolate that a dozen Snickers bars can never give you.

– Mireille Guiliano, Age, *15 January 2005*

The volume of food we eat has become a problem in many Western cultures. Our serving sizes are becoming bigger and we are eating faster. Many people live life at such a fast pace that they don't really taste their food. Mealtimes are treated as little more than a pit stop to refuel before racing back onto the track in search of the next thing. But slowing down can have real benefits, both for our relationship with food, our relationship with other people, and our relationship with ourselves. When we rush our food we are eating with very little awareness of how much and what we are eating. This means we are at risk of not only not enjoying what we eat but also not realising when we have had enough.

Action 4.9
How to slow down and enjoy your food

- Sit down. Try not to eat standing up or on the run.
- When you are eating just eat. Don't multitask and eat while reading, in front of the computer or when you are driving.
- Smell your food.
- Present the food attractively. Use your imagination.
- Chew your food properly. Your stomach doesn't have teeth.
- Pause between mouthfuls to make witty and charming dinner-table conversation.
- Be aware of how full you feel. Remember that it takes fifteen minutes for your brain to register that you are full.

10.

Food court: Deep-fried Chockers bars

On Saturday afternoon we all go to the movies to see *Giant Fighting Robot Man Saves the World*.

It is absolutely brilliant, of course, although I believe Mum and Dad made a huge mistake by refusing to take advantage of the $6.50 mega Zap! and giant popcorn deal offered with the tickets. Six dollars fifty!!! I guess some people just don't appreciate value when they see it.

After the movie we pass the food court.

There are shops selling every type of food imaginable. Nachos, pizza, hamburgers, Japanese, Chinese, fish and chips, sandwiches, souvlakis, baked potatoes, pizza, noodles, smoothies and ice-cream.

'I'm hungry,' I say. 'Can we get something to eat?'

Mum and Dad look at each other.

'What do you reckon?' says Dad. 'An early dinner?'

'Good idea,' says Mum, looking around. 'Oh, look – there's a Japanese place here. I might get some California rolls and some sushi.'

Dad makes a face. 'You can keep your raw fish. I'm going to have a steak sandwich with wedges and sour cream and a deep-fried Chockers bar for dessert.'

Mum rolls her eyes. 'Good healthy choice,' she says. 'Setting a great example for your son.'

Dad makes a face at me.

I laugh.

'You're right,' he says to Mum. 'I should be sensible. Guess I'll just have the deep-fried Chockers bar.'

'Closely followed by a heart attack,' says Mum. 'Jack?'

'I really feel like fish and chips,' I say, 'but they taste so good that I guess you won't let me have them.'

'Well,' she says, 'that all depends.'

'On what?' I say.

'On what you order and how much,' says Mum. 'If you have your fish grilled rather than deep-fried, and don't go crazy on the chips, it'll be fine.'

'Cool,' I say.

'I might have the same,' says Dad.

'And a can of Zap!?' I say.

'Have some water if you're thirsty,' says Mum.

'But Mum,' I say, looking around at the vast number of tables where a vast number of people are sitting down pouring a vast amount of Zap! down their throats, 'everybody else has got Zap!'

But Mum doesn't even bother looking. 'You know, Jack,' she says, 'I don't care what other people are eating or drinking. But I *do* care what *you* eat and drink because I care about you. I love you, Jack.'

'Shut up, Mum!' I say. 'You are SO embarrassing.'

Mum laughs and tries to kiss me.

I dodge. 'Come on, Dad,' I say. 'I've changed my mind. Let's go get our deep-fried Chockers bars.'

'What a good idea,' says Dad.

Nobody in the United States is forced to buy fast food. The first step toward meaningful change is by far the easiest: stop buying it. The executives who run the fast food industry are not bad men. They are businessmen. They will sell free-range, organic, grass-fed hamburgers if you demand it. They will sell whatever sells at a profit. The usefulness of the market, its effectiveness as a tool, cuts both ways. The real power of the American consumer has not yet been unleashed. The heads of Burger King, KFC, and McDonald's should feel daunted. There are three of them and almost three hundred million of

you. A good boycott, a refusal to buy, can speak much louder than words. Sometimes the most irresistible force is the most mundane.

– *Eric Schlosser,* Fast Food Nation

Healthy eating does not mean that you can't eat out, but it does mean being careful about what you choose to eat, and how much. Ultimately you are the one who decides what you put in your mouth. *You are in control*. Unfortunately, many people act as if the food is in control of them. You don't have to eat everything on your plate. You don't have to eat dessert just because everybody else is eating dessert. Healthy eating is about making consistently healthy choices, both in the quality of food you choose and the amount you choose to eat. Understand, however, that if you're making consistently good choices, the occasional slip-up or treat is not going to make much difference one way or another. It's just part of an overall healthy trend. You should find that when you're not eating junk on a regular basis, your taste for it will diminish accordingly. You can have your treat without going crazy. This goes for Christmas and various celebrations. Go with them, eat, enjoy . . . and then the next day continue to make your normal healthy choices.

Action 4.10
Making healthy choices when eating out

- Don't go to the restaurant hungry or starving. It will only encourage you to eat more than you really need. Your body requires food every three to four hours during the day – much better to feed it small amounts steadily throughout the day than to try to cram it all into a few meals.

- Ask for a glass of water at the table. Not only is it free, but it will help you to slow down.
- Consider ordering two entrées or an entrée and a salad rather than a main meal. Ask for dressings or sauces as a side dish so that you can control how much you use.
- Don't feel that you have to eat everything on your plate. For example, if your meal comes with chips you can have a few and enjoy them, but you don't have to eat all of them. If you can't do this, then ask for them not to be included with the dish. The point is to remember that you are in control at all times over what you put into your mouth – not the plate, not the waiter, not the chef, not the restaurant or your dining companions.
- Relax. Life is not a health camp. In the early stages of cleaning up your diet a certain amount of planning, determination and caution may be necessary and sensible. But when you've got things heading in the right direction, you can relax. Even when you have the best intentions, opportunities for treats will present themselves. Enjoy them.

11. In the park: A new world record?

Okay.

This is it.

I'm about to get in the *Guinness Book of World Records*.

Well, me and my dad.

Well, me and my dad and my *Aerobie Pro* flying ring. It's not just a Frisbee. It's better than that. Frisbees don't have a patented aerodynamic design and patented spoiler rim for stable, accurate flight. Mum bought it for me to encourage me not to swing on the clothesline.

'Okay!' yells Dad, standing on the other side of the park, 362 metres away. That's one metre more than the previous world's farthest throw. I don't want to break the record by too much. Not the first time, anyway. I don't want to be too much of a show-off.

We've been out after dinner most nights this week practising. It's surprisingly hard work.

Although the flying ring has stable, accurate flight, you can't always get it to go exactly where you want it to, so you end up spending a lot of time chasing, jumping and diving.

In fact it's almost more work than a session on the Miracle Skywalker. And you'd have to admit, a whole lot more fun.

But now we're ready.

It's time.

I stretch my throwing arm.

I kiss the flying ring, take a deep breath and throw it as hard as I can.

It sails through the air, rising and dipping on invisible currents towards my dad. Towards my destiny. Who wants to be a TV chef anyway? This is bigger than that. Way bigger.

There's only one problem.

My flying ring is no longer heading towards Dad.

Well, it sort of is, but it's going way over his head.

Towards a row of pine trees at the edge of the park!

It disappears into the middle of the tallest tree.

Oh no!

This is terrible!

I've broken the world record, but if we lose the flying ring I won't be able to send it to the *Guinness Book of World Records* office in London for verification.

I run across the park to Dad.

He's standing underneath the tree looking up. 'I can see it,' he says, pointing to one of the highest branches.

'We've got to get it down,' I say. 'We've *got* to!'

'Okay, okay,' says Dad. 'Calm down. We'll try to knock it out with pine cones.'

'Good idea,' I say. We each pick up a handful of pine cones and start hurling them at the flying ring.

But it's no use. It's up too high.

There's only one thing for it.

'Dad,' I say, 'give me a booster. I'm going up.'

This is *definitely* more fun than the Skywalker.

A few months ago I suggested to my mate . . . 'How 'bout we go throw the Frizz?' and we went to the park with a dodgy little Frisbee and had a great time. Then I remembered that when I was young I had 'one of those Ring Things that go a footy field' and I wanted another one! The first time we got out there

with the Aerobie Pro ring I was knackered. After a lazy winter, chasing that thing took it out of me. Months later Marcus and I are bloody pros! And I ache to finish work early, grab the ring, head to the field and . . . and now this is where I'm lost for words. Nothing can describe the enjoyment and peace I get from those days. Maybe I just love running barefoot in the grass with the spring sun setting, but there's more to it than that. With the Pro ring I get so much exercise, then there's agility, prediction, coordination and so much laughter when all you and passers by can say is, 'That's Bloody Amazing.' And so many people come and join in . . . kids, then their parents. Now they have their own rings. People drop their kites to come have a go. Now even my dear ol' Dad comes down with us and brings the dog – thank you, he needs the exercise.

– Glenn Harrison, Melbourne, Australia

There are many negative connotations around the word 'exercise'. But exercise doesn't have to be 'exercise'. Better to think of it as 'movement'. If conventional exercise equipment works for you and you enjoy it, then go for it. But there are many other alternatives. Just because you or your child are not participating in a conventionally structured sporting game, it doesn't mean that you are not moving.

Action 4.11
Alternatives to 'conventional' exercise

- In the park:
  - Frisbees and flying rings
  - hide and seek
  - playgrounds
  - piggy-back races
  - kite-flying
  - kick to kick
  - roller blading
  - tennis balls
  - all types of chasing games (scarecrow, bob-down, etc. Make up your own variations, e.g. crying chasey, zombie chasey, dancing chasey, rude sounds chasey)
- In the backyard:
  - skipping
  - making cubby houses
  - garden work
  - billycarts, bike-riding and skate boarding
  - sprinkler
  - paddlepool
  - sandplt
  - tree-climbing
  - dancing
- At the beach:
  - swimming
  - sandcastle-building
  - volleyball
  - fishing
  - cricket
  - rockpooling
  - board-riding
  - hopscotch
- See also Action 5.7, 'Simple resources for encouraging inside play' on page 268.

12. Planning the weekend: Ghost train vs bloodsucking leeches

'What are we doing today, Mum?' I say, as the prospect of another endless Saturday without TV or computer games stretches in front of me.

'I don't know,' says Mum, who is busy making toast. But not proper toast. Brown bread toast.

'Can we go to the movies?' I say.

'I don't know,' says Mum. 'I was thinking of something a little more active . . .'

'We could go and see an action movie,' I say. 'They're active.'

'The actors are active,' says Mum, 'but you're not doing anything.'

'Yes, I am,' I say.

'What?' says Mum, rolling her eyes, putting a sad piece of brown bread toast on my plate.

'Um,' I say. 'Watching the movie. That's something.'

'But it's not much,' says Mum.

'I'm sitting,' I say, desperately. 'And breathing. And action movies really get my heart pumping. That's hardly "not doing anything".'

'Yes,' says Mum. 'But it's *hardly* anything. I want you to get out there and run around. And you don't need that much butter for one piece of toast!'

'I do,' I say. 'I'm trying to cover up the fact that it's brown.'

Mum shakes her head, takes the knife out of my hand and returns most of the butter to the dish. Then she hands the knife back to me.

'What am I supposed to do with this?' I say. 'This is hardly enough to cover my fingernail!'

'That's more than enough butter for one piece of toast,' says Mum.

I scrape the sad amount of butter onto my sad piece of toast. But as I'm doing it, I have a brain flash. 'What about Luna Park?' I suggest. 'We could run from ride to ride and there's a new ghost train and . . .'

'How about we drive up to Sherbrooke Forest and hike to the waterfalls?' says Dad.

'What a good idea!' says Mum. 'We can take a picnic.'

'That's a *dumb* idea,' I say, rolling my eyes.

'Why?' says Dad.

'Because we'll miss out on the ghost train,' I say.

'You can go to that anytime,' says Dad.

'You can go to the Sherbrooke Falls anytime, too,' I say.

'How about when we get home we turn all the lights off and I put a white sheet over my head and you give me five dollars and I'll chase you around the house?' says Dad.

'That's an even *dumber* idea,' I say, laughing. 'The ghost train at Luna Park only costs *three* dollars!'

'How about we stop off at Luna Park on the way home from Sherbrooke Forest and go on the ghost train then?' says Mum.

'How about we stop off at Luna Park on the way to Sherbrooke Forest and give Sherbrooke Forest a miss?' I say.

'No,' says Mum firmly.

'But what about the leeches?' I say.

'What about them?' says Dad.

'They suck your blood, Dad,' I say. 'They crawl up your trouser legs and sink their fangs into your ankles and your thighs and even your . . .'

'That sounds better than the ghost train,' says Mum. 'Much scarier.'

'All right,' I say. 'But don't say I didn't warn you. I just don't see the point of getting exercise if you end up as a bloodless corpse covered in leeches.'

'There will be no bloodless corpses covered in leeches,' says Mum. 'We're going and that's final.'

I shrug, pick up my toast and have a bite. Actually, it's not as bad as I thought. Not as bad as being sucked dry by Sherbrooke Forest leeches, anyway.

If you want to achieve a healthy weight, stop wanting to lose weight and start wanting those things – an active life, good food, and the calm enjoyment of both – that, unlike weight loss are unalloyed goods in and of themselves. If you can manage to do this, you may well lose weight in the process; but far more important, you will get to a place where the weight you lose has been lost precisely because you no longer care, at some deep level of self-acceptance, whether you've lost weight or not.

– *Paul Campos,* The Obesity Myth

A family activity or outing can be a great opportunity for both spending time together and moving. Be imaginative. Get out a map and look for opportunities that you may not have noticed. There are usually great places for active family outings less than a hour away from home – either by car or train. Include the family in negotiating where to go. Take a picnic. Make it fun.

Action 4.12
Active family outings

- While you will no doubt find favourite family spots, occasionally – say, once a month – make a point of going somewhere that you've never been before.
- Create a family outing book – a blank sketch pad is ideal – to keep a record of your adventures. You don't need much . . . a couple of photos, ticket stubs, pressed flowers, funny comments or incidents, brief thoughts. It can provide a lot of pleasure to read through, and a good motivation for creating new adventures. Keep a page at the back for adding ideas about where to go next.
- Places to go: adventure playgrounds, beach, bowling alley, ice/roller skating centre, climbing centres, swimming pools, national parks, bicycle paths/tracks.
- Simple picnic foods: bottles of water, dried fruit/nut mix, sandwiches, dips, bread, cut-up vegetables, pieces of whole fruit, cake, etc.

13. Sherbrooke Forest: Back to nature

I'm sitting on a rock at the edge of Sherbrooke Falls, dangling my feet in the water.

It's cold but we've been walking for over an hour and a half, and my feet are aching. Around us are huge ancient tree ferns, moss-covered boulders and the roar of the falls.

So far there is no sign of killer bloodsucking leeches, but I keep checking my legs just to be sure.

Dad is swatting at flies with the branch of a gum tree.

'Did we bring anything to eat?' I say. 'Some muesli bars or chips or something? I'm starving.'

Mum reaches into her day pack and hands me a plastic bag. 'Have some scroggin,' she says.

Uh-oh.

More health food with a strange name.

'Scroggin?' says Dad. 'What on earth is that?'

'Try it and see,' says Mum, mysteriously.

I open the top of the bag. I can't believe it! It's full of nuts, seeds, dried fruit and, best of all, chips of dark chocolate.

I take a big handful and put it in my mouth.

It's beautiful.

You know, I reckon I could get used to health food. Especially if they put chocolate chips in everything. Well, except for the salads. That would probably be a bit disgusting. Then again, this tastes so good that it would definitely be worth a try.

'I'm thirsty,' I say.

'Have some water,' says Dad.

'Where's the tap?' I say, looking around.

Mum laughs. 'There's no tap,' she says. 'You can drink from the falls.'

'Really?' I say. 'Is it safe?'

'Of course it's safe,' says Dad.

'What about the leeches?' I say.

'We'll keep a lookout for you,' he says.

'Thanks,' I say. I kneel down close to the water and scoop a handful into my mouth.

The water splashes down my chin and all over my T-shirt.

I lie back and look up at the clouds through the gentle curtain of mist thrown up by the falls.

The sun feels warm on my face.

A small bird makes a sound as clear and piercing as a bell in the tree above us.

I've never heard a bird make that sound. I didn't know they could.

I grab another big handful of scroggin.

And listen.

We tend to think of air, food, and water as the three essentials for life. We forget there could be no life on earth without sunlight. Although our knowledge in this area is in a very early stage, indirect sun rays come through the eyes and affect the pineal gland and its production of melatonin. This in turn affects or governs the hypothalamus and through the hypothalamus the endocrine systems of the body. As a basic guideline, it is desirable for everyone to spend at least one hour per day out-of-doors, but it is especially important for children to do so.

– *J. Liberman,* Light, Medicine of the Future

Despite the complexity of modern life in the West, the simple things remain the most important. Air, food, water and sunlight. And they're yours any time you want them . . . all you have to do is to open a door and step outside.

Action 4.13
Natural living

- Aim to spend at least one hour out-of-doors each day. (Take basic safety precautions against sunburn.)
- Take a few moments to make yourself aware of your body. Feel your fingers. Feel your toes. Notice how you are sitting. Feel the life in your body.
- Take a few deep breaths of fresh air to expand your lungs fully.
- Eat natural unprocessed foods whenever possible. Remember that the closer your food is to its original state in nature, the more nutritious and the better for you it is.
- Drink a glass of water – slowly. Many people fail to drink enough water. Coffee, tea and alcohol all deplete the body of water. Aim to drink between six and eight glasses of water every day. Children will learn to enjoy water, particularly if they see their parents drink it and when it is the only drink on offer.

14. Turning the TV off: Taking control

It's over.

Giant Fighting Robot Man has saved the world again.

Which is good.

But what is *not* good is that my hour of television is over.

It's cruel.

I have to wait a whole 23 hours before I can turn it on again.

I watch right to the end of the credits. Right to the end of the last note of music. Right to the last logo.

And then it's over.

I have to turn it off now.

But I *can't*.

There's a preview of tomorrow's episode. I watch it. Giant Fighting Robot Man is fighting Giant Fighting Robot Monster!

Cool!

Now I've definitely got to turn it off.

I have my finger poised over the red button on the remote.

But I hesitate for a moment too long and an ad for Lotza Pizza! comes on. Now hang on, this is interesting. Two pizzas and a 2-litre bottle of Zap! for $10.99! That's practically giving it away.

I've got to call Mum.

I'm sure she'd be willing to make an exception to our healthy diet. Just this once, at least. Especially when she finds out how cheap it is!

I'm looking around the room for the phone when an ad for *Survivor* comes on. The contestants are walking through a crocodile-infested swamp! Now that I've got to see! But it's on tonight and I've already used my hour of TV. There's no way . . .

Unless . . .

I dig out the video recorder manual.

I can time-shift it!

The manual is complicated, but I'm desperate.

By the time I've figured it out the next program has started.

It's a game show that I haven't seen before.

But I can't keep watching.

I have to turn it off.

But I can't.

But I must.

Rusty is pawing at the door. I usually take him for a walk around this time and he's leaping and slobbering with anticipation.

With a mighty effort of will I manage to push the little red button all the way in.

I did it!

The screen goes dark.

The room falls silent.

Well, except for Rusty's racket.

But I'll soon fix that.

When people say to me – 'How do you do so many things?' I often answer them, without meaning to be cruel – 'How do you do so little?' It seems to me that people have a vast potential. Most people can do extraordinary things if they have the confidence or take the risks. Yet most people don't. They sit in front of the telly and treat life as if it goes on forever.

– Phillip Adams

An important, and often overlooked, component of health is the feeling of being in control of your life. Not having control over significant parts of your life, your work, your family, your habits, your emotions, your diet or your finances can all take a tremendous toll on your health. There are few things more satisfying – for both children and adults – than gaining mastery of a particular skill or activity. The pride of achievement builds your self-esteem, which in turn lays the foundation for further mastery. And one of the most important – and for many the most difficult – skills to master is turning the TV off when you've finished watching the program that you turned it on for.

Action 4.14
How to gain at least two to three hours a day to put towards activities that make you feel happier and healthier

- Turn off the television.
- Turn off the television.
- Turn off the television.
- Turn off the television.
- Turn off the television.

Part 5

A Day in Jack's New Life

1.

Waking up: Get up and go

I can hear birds.

I open my eyes.

It's not day yet, but it's not night either.

I look across at my clock.

6.00 am.

I read until 6.30 am, when I hear Rusty whining.

I get up, pull on a T-shirt, tracksuit pants and runners and slip quietly out the back door.

It's cold. I'm breathing out great clouds of mist. Rusty hears me and emerges from his kennel. He sees the leash in my hand and starts jumping up onto me.

I clip the leash onto his chain, grab my skateboard and we're away.

He's so happy to be out he's towing me down the street.

'Slow down, Rusty!' I say.

But Rusty speeds up.

He's not listening to me anymore.

Rusty has seen a cat.

We hurtle down the street.

The cat scoots up and over a wooden paling fence. Rusty screeches to a screaming halt. I keep going, lose my balance and end up face-first in the nature strip.

I sit up spitting dirt and grass.

My skateboard is upside down, its wheels still spinning. Mum was right. These things *are* dangerous.

Rusty is going crazy trying to get through the fence so that he can catch the cat.

He's pushing his nose into the gap beneath the bottom of the fence and digging a hole through the footpath.

I pick myself up, grab the end of Rusty's leash and try to haul him away. 'Good try, Rusty,' I say. 'Better luck next time.'

Now it's my turn to tow Rusty down the street.

Outside the milk bar I tie him up and go inside.

Mr Holybon gives me a big smile. 'Morning, Jack,' he says. 'The usual?'

'Yep,' I say, handing him three coins. I grab a carton of milk and a newspaper from the pile next to the door. 'See you tomorrow!'

Rusty, recovered from his cat-chase, tows me home on my skateboard.

After nearly getting my head knocked off by a low-lying branch and almost losing my skateboard down a stormwater drain, we arrive home, both panting out great clouds of early-morning mist.

A trip to the milk bar with Rusty is almost more exciting than watching *Giant Fighting Robot Man*.

Well . . . almost.

Sleep is fundamental to a healthy immune system, sound mental health and the growth and repair of every cell in the body.

– *Sheila Lavery,* The Healing Power of Sleep

Eating well, playing well and sleeping well give a feeling of vitality. Sleep is a natural response to physical tiredness. If a child – or an adult – does not do much physical exercise during the day, they may be mentally tired, but not physically tired when they go to bed. Lack of sleep leads to a vicious circle in which the body is not fully replenished, which leads to a lack of vitality, low energy levels, and even less inclination to exercise.

Action 5.1
Sleeping for better health

- Ensure regular bedtime hours for your child. On average children aged from six to ten years require ten hours' sleep per night. Eleven- to thirteen-year-olds require 9.5 hours. Adults require around eight hours for optimal health.

- Establish a bedtime routine. This helps to prepare children (and adults) for the transition from activity to rest, e.g. dinner, bath/shower, reading in bed, lights out.
- Getting a minimum of 30 to 45 minutes of exercise helps you to become physically tired and ensures better sleep. Don't think of it as an optional extra. Think of it as one of the most important parts of your day.
- Avoid drinks containing caffeine before bed if you have difficulty sleeping. Caffeine is a stimulant and can take twelve hours to metabolise in some people. Coffee and cola drinks contain large amounts of caffeine.
- Bedtime is an opportune time to listen to your child. During the daytime they may not talk about any concerns they have. Often just talking about a problem and bringing it to awareness can be a great relief and prevent the child from brooding on it after lights out.
- Concentrating on relaxing music with your eyes shut can be a very pleasant way of encouraging your brain and body to relax and drift off to sleep.

2.

Breakfast: Record-breaking boy

I stand in the kitchen and look in the cupboard.

No Chockoes. No Rainbow Rocks. No Endurocrunch.

Just rolled oats. But that's okay.

I pour out a cupful into a saucepan, add two cups of water and bring it to the boil. Pretty soon it's thick and steaming. I scoop a couple of cups into my bowl, add a sprinkling of dried fruit and nuts and pour milk over the top.

'Good morning, Jack,' says Mum, puffing slightly as she enters the kitchen.

'Morning, Mum,' I say. 'Nice walk?'

'Beautiful,' she says. 'Not a breath of wind.'

'Would you like some porridge?' I say.

'That would be lovely,' says Mum. She sits down

at the table and opens the newspaper while I prepare another bowl.

'Look at this, Jack!' says Mum, as I put the bowls on the table.

'What?' I say.

'The Aerobie Pro Ring record has been broken!' says Mum.

I splutter a mouthful of porridge and milk all over the newspaper. 'You're kidding!' I say. 'Who? When? How far?'

'Eric Hemmings threw an Aerobie Pro Ring 406 metres,' reads Mum, 'breaking the old record of 361 by 45 metres!'

'That's nothing!' I say. 'I've thrown further than that. And if we could have got the ring out of the tree I would have been able to prove it and that would be *my* record.'

'That's too bad, Jack,' says Mum.

'Yeah,' I say. 'But I'll take care of it.'

Eric Hemmings has got another thing coming if he thinks he's going to hang on to that record for very long.

I'm going back into training for another world record attempt. And this time there will be no mistakes.

I finish my porridge, grab the bread and make a chicken sandwich. I put it in my lunch box along with an apple, a yoghurt and a handful of nuts.

I haven't got a minute to waste. I've got to get to school and start practising.

I shower and get dressed.

I put on the new windcheater I got for my birthday, but it doesn't look right with my pants.

I change my pants and it's fine.

I go into the bathroom, brush my teeth and gel my hair. It takes a few goes until I get it the way I like it, but it finally spikes up just right.

I get my new flying ring, put it into my bag along with my lunch box and grab my bike helmet.

'See you later, Mum,' I say as I head out the door.

'Hang on,' says Mum. 'You forgot something.'

'What?' I say.

'This,' she says, giving me a big squeeze.

'Mum!' I say. 'That's really nice and everything, but I can't stand around here hugging all day . . . I've got a record to break!'

Mum nods, smiles and lets go. 'Good luck,' she says. 'May the force be with you.'

'Thanks, Mum,' I say. 'May the force be with you.'

I walk down the steps. Mum's much happier since she went part-time, but she's no less crazy.

Primary school aged children, when asked, 'Name one thing you would like your mum and dad to

give you this Christmas that would not cost a penny' answered as follows:

1. **Listen to me please**
2. **Teach me how to cook**
3. **Please stop smoking**
4. **Stop being so busy all the time**
5. **Read to me**
6. **Hug me more.**

– Adapted from Linda Sharp, 'All I want for Christmas . . . Parents you may be surprised'

Rushing around in the morning is so familiar to many of us that we don't question whether it could be any other way, or whether there's anything particularly wrong with it. But it's worth asking how we can slow down in the mornings and make deeper connections with ourselves, our bodies, our food and each other. Not only is our morning more enjoyable when we do so, but it sets us up for a heightened sense of health and wellbeing throughout the day.

Action 5.2
Ensuring a healthy and enjoyable start to the day

- Do some sort of activity – walking, jogging, riding, or simply take a few minutes to stretch and reconnect with your body.
- Eat a healthy breakfast. Encourage your child to do the same. Better still, encourage them to make a healthy breakfast for you.

- Plan ahead to make sure you have the foods available so that you – and your child – can prepare simple, healthy lunches for yourselves with a minimum of fuss.
- Think creatively about ways to reduce or eliminate the 'rush' of your mornings. Entertain the possibility that there is no 'rush' except for the 'rush' that you have created for yourselves, and that it is possible to begin to 'uncreate' it.
- Discuss with your child the night before what is happening the next day. If they are prepared for what is going on they can be helpful rather than confused and resistant.
- Hug! Hold the hug for a few seconds or longer. Repeat.

3. Skating to school: In the land of the fast

I'm bent down low on my skateboard, cruising smoothly along the footpath.

Well, pretty smoothly except for the clackety-clack of the skateboard wheels against the gaps and cracks in the concrete.

I smile as I begin to pick up speed down the slope that leads to Jeremy's house. The red skeleton head on top of my skateboard grins back at me. We're really moving now. And this morning we're going to win.

I can see Jeremy waiting out the front of his house, his foot poised on his skateboard. I swoop down the hill towards him and tag his hand as I speed past.

It's on.

I've got the advantage on him, but a glance behind me reveals that he's rapidly gaining ground.

I pump the ground madly with my right foot, accelerating somewhere close to the speed of light.

But it's not enough.

Jeremy is travelling *at* the speed of light.

He draws alongside me, a grin on his face wider than the one on the red skull.

'So long,' he says, drawing ahead of me.

'I don't think so,' I say, pumping harder than ever and drawing level with him. The rest of the world is a blur as we speed along, side by side.

Nothing exists except for us, the red skull and the crackety-crack of the skateboards as we tear up the footpath.

This is better than driving to school with Mum.

This is better than PlayStation.

This is even better than *Giant Fighting Robot Man: The Movie*.

Sure, at 86,000 kilometres an hour our lives are on the line, but it doesn't matter.

This is real.

We fell out of trees, got cut and broke bones and teeth, and there were no lawsuits from these accidents. They were accidents. No-one was to

blame but us. We would spend hours building our go-carts out of scraps and then ride down the hill, only to find out we forgot the brakes. After running into the bushes a few times, we learned to solve the problem. This generation (the over 35's) has produced some of the best risk-takers and problem solvers and inventors, ever.

– *Anonymous, 'People over 35 should be dead'*

Cardiovascular disease is the number one killer of Australians. As a society we have learned to 'buckle up' and not 'drink and drive' and we all know that 'speed kills', but the number of deaths per year from road accidents is only a fraction of the number of deaths per year from cardiovascular disease and obesity-related illness.

We wouldn't dream of letting a child travel in a car without a seatbelt, but we think nothing of leaving them for hours in front of a television or computer. Sure, there's an element of risk riding skateboards. But there's an element of risk in anything, when it comes down to it. The crucial thing is to keep the risk in perspective and to ask ourselves whether the risk of not doing the activity might, in fact, outweigh the risk of doing it.

A sedentary lifestyle is 'safer' in terms of avoiding injury than an active lifestyle, but this short-term 'safety' comes at a high long-term cost. A vastly increased risk of obesity, heart disease, cardiovascular disease, diabetes and a lack of vitality are just a few of the predictable outcomes of a sedentary lifestyle. The short- and long-term benefits of a sustained skills-based activity such as skateboard-riding, however, are numerous.

Cardiovascular fitness, balance, flexibility, strength and sheer exhilaration are all absolutely guaranteed. For children to gain independence, confidence and strength we need to be able to let them go.

Action 5.3
Keeping risk in perspective

- Assess your child's maturity and readiness before agreeing to their taking part in a particular activity.
- Remember that life cannot be lived 'risk-free', however much we may pretend – and wish – that it were otherwise.
- Keep in mind that a sedentary lifestyle may be a far greater risk to the long-term physical and mental health of your child than the risk of a few bruises and broken bones.
- Encourage your child to take appropriate safety measures: helmet, knee and elbow pads, etc.
- Introduce some risk into your own life. Be a role model for your child.

4. In class: Maths Brain challenge Part 2

It's Friday afternoon and we're playing Mr Fitzgerald's weekly 'Maths Brain' challenge.

Our group is ahead by one point.

One point ahead of Dean's group.

We only need to get the next answer right and the title will be ours. Not to mention that the Maths Brain trophy will be ours for the week.

I feel something wet hit the back of my neck.

I turn around. Dean's eyes are turned towards the ceiling.

'Grow up, Dean,' I say.

'What?' he says. 'What are you talking about?'

'You're a dork, Dean,' I say.

He smirks. 'I'm not the one with a spitball on the back of my neck,' he says.

'That's because you don't have a neck,' I say. 'Neanderthal.'

Dean frowns. I can see he doesn't know what 'Neanderthal' means. But he knows it's not good.

'All right,' says Mr Fitzgerald. 'Last question.'

I lean forwards to make sure I hear every word of it. So do Jeremy and Alice. But Sophie . . . well, Sophie is just drawing flowers on her folder.

'The pizza was cut into ten even pieces,' says Mr Fitzgerald. 'Betty ate half of the pizza. Dave ate two-tenths. Brenda ate one-quarter. How many pieces were left for John? Three minutes. Go!'

'I hate pizza questions,' says Jeremy.

'I hate pizza,' says Alice.

'What do you think of this flower?' says Sophie.

'Come on, guys,' I say. 'Don't you want to win?'

'Yes,' says Jeremy. 'But how? This problem is impossible!'

'No it's not,' I say. I pull Sophie's folder into the middle of the table. 'Look,' I say. 'This flower has ten petals. Imagine each of these petals is a slice of pizza. Betty ate half so that's five pieces, or petals in this case. So we colour in five petals.'

'No, don't,' says Sophie. 'You'll wreck it.'

'I'm not going to wreck it,' I say. 'Colouring it in will make it even better.'

'Yeah, see,' says Alice, picking up a pen and helping me shade in five petals.

'Colour in two more,' says Jeremy, 'because Dave ate two-tenths.'

Sophie pulls the folder away from Alice and starts colouring. 'I should do it,' she says. 'After all, it's my flower.'

'Brenda ate one-quarter,' I say. 'So what's a quarter of ten?'

We all study the flower.

'Any ideas?' I say.

'No,' says Jeremy. 'Beats me.'

'No,' says Alice blankly.

'Two point five,' says Sophie. She colours in two petals then carefully draws a line through the middle of the last petal and colours in one half.

I study the flower. She's right.

'Which leaves half a piece for John,' I say.

'That's not fair,' says Alice.

'Who cares?' I say, putting my hand up to signal to Mr Fitzgerald. 'We've won.'

I turn around and smirk at Dean.

Recent research demonstrates a direct link between fitness and intelligence, particularly in children under sixteen . . . The truth is that the domains of child development – physical, social, emotional, and cognitive – simply do not mature separately from

one another. There's an overlap and interrelatedness among them. And children do not differentiate among thinking, feeling, and moving. Thus, when a child learns something related to one domain, it impacts on others.

Rae Pica, Your Active Child

Our minds are not separate from our bodies. How we move and care for our bodies affects how we think. How we think affects how we feel. How we feel affects how we relate to ourselves and others. And how we relate to ourselves and others affects our physical health in very powerful ways that researchers are only just beginning to understand. Improvements in one area of our lives will have flow-on benefits for all of the others.

Action 5.4
Balanced development

Physical

Make it your business to ensure that your child is provided with the opportunity for between 30 and 60 minutes of moderately vigorous activity most days of the week. Plan ahead to make a variety of fresh, unprocessed foods available for them to eat. Don't just assume that these things will happen by themselves – in the current environment it's safer to assume they might not.

Social

Balance time spent alone with time spent relating to other people. Children will not necessarily know how to regulate their use of solitary computer games and television watching and may need you to set – and enforce – guidelines.

Emotional

Encourage your child to become sensitive to and aware of their feelings. When they talk about their feelings try not to judge, advise or criticise. Just listen and help them to understand what's going on inside them. Spending time helping your child get to know themselves will not only help their development but will also help them to better understand and relate to others.

Cognitive

To enjoy optimum health, an active brain is as important as an active body. Challenge your brain – and your children's brains – in lots of different ways, e.g. wooden puzzles, jigsaw puzzles, word games, making things, dancing and simply playing. But don't forget to relax. Give yourself – and your children – time out to simply 'be' without doing, thinking or worrying about anything in particular. Creating this time makes space to move your mental furniture into new, unexpected and possibly more effective patterns.
And it feels good.

5. Lunchtime: Sandwiches, salads and fresh fruit

The lunch basket arrives from the canteen.

It fills the room with the smell of hot chicken salad.

The canteen doesn't sell pies or pasties or even hot dogs anymore. It's part of the school's new policy on healthy eating. It's all sandwiches and salads and fresh fruit.

The first lunch bell rings.

I get my lunch box from my bag and sit back down at my desk.

We have to spend the first ten minutes of lunch eating in the classrooms now. It's part of the school's new healthy eating policy. They figure that if we're actually sitting down inside, we're more likely to eat our lunches.

Not that you can buy chips or Cheesy Chunks from the canteen anymore.

I eat my sandwich, yoghurt and apple. I'm just brushing the crumbs off my desk when the second bell rings.

There's a stampede for the door.

I grab one handle of the class sports bag and Jeremy grabs the other. As part of the school's overhaul on physical education and movement every class has been given its own bag full of sports equipment. No more searching the school for Mr Smith. Jeremy and I are the sports bag monitors for the week. It's our job to make sure all the stuff that belongs to our class gets put back in the bag.

We head over to the playing field and dump the bag on the grass.

Some kids grab the cricket gear. Others take the football. A few of the girls grab a box of chalk and start drawing hopscotch squares on the bitumen.

Jeremy and I take a Frisbee each.

I go up one end of the field and he goes up the other end and we begin throwing them to each other.

We're not too bad with our distance and accuracy, but it's like the Frisbees have minds of their own. We spend most of the next 40 minutes sprinting, jumping and laughing as they do their best to evade us.

In fact, it's so much work that we're almost glad when the bell rings.

We collect up the gear in the bag, lug it back up the hill and stop off at the water taps for a long cold drink.

Did I mention that we can't buy lemonade at the canteen anymore? It's part of the school's new healthy drinking policy.

We as a society have really abdicated responsibility for teaching kids how to eat right and how to have an active lifestyle. Promoting their physical well-being should be part of the school's educational mission.

– *Dr David Ludwig,* Time, *28 June 2004*

Both parents and teachers need to support initiatives for changes in schools. The food sold at school needs to reflect the types of foods that children are taught in school they should be eating. There is no point spending the morning discussing the food pyramid if at lunchtime the kids can buy a pie and a can of soft drink at the canteen. A policy on healthy eating sets clear boundaries. It also takes pressure off parents who might otherwise succumb to their children's demands for junk food due to peer pressure.

Action 5.5
What schools can do

- Schools should offer nutritious and appealing food to students at the school canteen, in classroom food activities, and at other events such as school camps, dances and fundraising events. They need to remove junk food from the menu and normalise nutritious food that feeds the brain and body and doesn't overload it with sugar and fat.
- Don't encourage the use of food as rewards or to deal with emotions, as this can set up unhealthy patterns of eating for comfort rather than directly expressing emotions. Positive behaviour can be rewarded using other incentives, e.g. free play, awards, choosing an activity.
- Encourage students to enjoy and really taste the food they eat. Remember food not only nourishes us but also gives us immense pleasure and is an important part of our social lives. Set aside ten to fifteen minutes for students to eat and enjoy their lunches, sitting down, before they leave the classroom for lunchtime activities.
- Grow sprouts, lettuce and tomatoes to eat. They could be grown in the classroom in trays or in pots outside. Better still, set up a community garden for the whole school.
- Look for ways to incorporate food and cooking into the curriculum. For instance, measurement and quantities can be taught in mathematics by giving students the opportunity to follow a simple recipe.
- Organise a freely available sports bag for each classroom with a range of equipment both for competitive sports

(footy, cricket, soccer, etc.) and non-competitive sports (skipping ropes, hopscotch chalk, Frisbees, etc.).

- Use a recipe to make simple dishes. Cooking may not necessarily be required, e.g. fruit salads, dry biscuits with toppings.
- Spend time outside the classroom. Measure areas around the school. Use jugs and buckets for estimating volumes of water.
- Contact the Nutrition Australia School Advisory Service at www.nutritionaustralia.org for more information about how your school can make a difference.

6.
PE class: I love sport!

I'm bent over.

Panting.

A red ball is hurtling down a tunnel of legs towards me.

I catch it, sprint up to the front of the line, bend over and throw it back through my legs as hard as I can.

Alice catches the ball at the end and sprints to the front.

Mr Smith blows his whistle.

'All change!' he yells. 'Skipping!'

We all sprint to the other side of the yard and pick up skipping ropes.

Mr Smith blows his whistle. 'One minute warm-up,' he says. 'Then 30 seconds flat out!'

I pick up the rope and start skipping.

I used to be really bad at this. I could never get more than two or three skips before the skipping rope tangled around my legs. But now I can go for at least a whole minute.

Mr Smith blows his whistle again. 'Thirty seconds flat out. Pick up the pace!'

I start skipping as fast as I can.

It seems like I'm only just getting started when Mr Smith blows his whistle again and tells us to do as many push-ups as we can in 30 seconds.

I drop the rope, lie down on the ground and put my hands out to the side.

I push up.

One. No problems.

Two. Okay.

Three. Starting to feel it.

Four. Definitely feeling it now.

Five. Starting to hurt.

Six. Definitely hurting. But I think I can go one more.

Seven. Really, really hurting . . .

I drop to my knees and do three half push-ups before Mr Smith blows his whistle.

'Good work, Jack,' he says to me. 'You'll be doing ten full push-ups soon. Just concentrate on doing one extra one each time we do this.'

I nod, wiping sweat out of my eyes.

'All right, everybody,' says Mr Smith. 'Enough warm-up. Bob-down tiggy! Jack's it. Go!'

I take off and touch as many people as I can. I leave a swathe of bobbed-down people behind me, but as fast as I can get them to bob down, the free agents tag and release them.

Just when I reckon I can't run anymore Mr Smith blows his whistle. 'Stretching!' he says. 'I want you to lie on the floor and make your body as long as possible. Really stretch out!'

I lie down on my stomach and try to touch the opposite wall with my fingers.

This is what I love most about Mr Smith's PE classes.

You never know what's going to happen next.

If you were offered a program that enhanced your child's physical and mental health, academic performance, social development, and self-concept, would you turn it down? What if it also promoted an appreciation for life-long physical activity, and there was no additional charge above and beyond what you are already paying for your child's schooling?

Such a program exists. And, surprisingly, parents have been known to reject it – sometimes even vehemently.

It's called physical education.

– *Rae Pica,* Your Active Child

PE classes should be fun. Children can learn new games, using skills which they are physically ready for and developmentally capable of. Remember, PE improves thinking and academic performance; it should not be seen as an optional extra to the curriculum.

Action 5.6
Features to look for in an effective PE class

- There should be an emphasis on active movement. Skills acquisition and competition are important – and can be very enjoyable for many children – but should not be the main focus of the class.
- Variety: a mixture of low-intensity movement (cardio) and high-intensity movement (strength).
- Activities where each child can participate at their own level.
- Fun and enjoyable activities that have the effect of encouraging a lifelong love of physical activity.

7. After school: Giant Fighting Robot Monster Attack

Giant Fighting Robot Man grunts as his massive body hits the wall. Cracks appear in the bricks and the entire wall crumbles to the ground. Giant Fighting Robot Man picks himself up. 'You'll pay for that, Robot Monster!' he says, hurling himself through the air at his mortal enemy.

He lands on top of the Robot Monster and starts karate-chopping him to a bloody pulp, but the monster refuses to die. He gets up and pile-drives Giant Fighting Robot Man into a deep hole in the ground.

Oh no!

If he doesn't stop soon he'll smash him into the centre of the earth and crack the planet in half!

I can't bear it.

I put my hands up to surrender.

'No, Jeremy!' I say. 'No! That hurts! Stop!'

'Robot Monster will never stop,' says Jeremy. 'Giant Fighting Robot Monster shows no mercy.'

'Help!' I yell across the yard to Rusty, who is lying on his mat. 'Giant Fighting Robot Dog! Help me!'

But Giant Fighting Robot Dog does not come to his master's aid. Giant Fighting Robot Dog is a giant fighting robotic dud!

I'll deal with him later.

Meanwhile, Jeremy keeps pounding me.

I manage to roll out from underneath him and grab a long stick from the garden. I hold it above my head in two hands. 'Behold the sword of power!' I say.

Robot Monster's face contorts in terror and he shields his face from the sword.

'Not the sword of power!' he says. 'Anything but that!'

'It's too late for you now, Robot Monster!' I say. 'Next time you decide to enslave a planet, remember the sword of power!'

Robot Monster's only response is to run screaming down the driveway.

I chase him as far as the letter box. 'You hungry?' I say.

'You bet,' he says.

I drop the stick and go back up the drive towards the back door. I nudge Rusty with my foot. He looks up at me. 'Some help you turned out to be,' I say.

'I can't believe you didn't realise he was a double agent,' says Jeremy. 'He's been working for me all along.'

Jeremy stoops to pat Rusty's head.

Rusty growls and Jeremy withdraws his hand quickly.

'That might be true,' I say. 'But he likes me better.'

Inside we make a smoothie with strawberries and bananas.

It's not that we're trying to be particularly healthy or anything – it's all we can find. And it tastes good.

'I'd better be getting home,' says Jeremy. 'Can we do this again after school tomorrow?'

'Haven't you learnt your lesson yet, Giant Fighting Robot Monster?' I say.

'Yes,' he says, 'but I don't think you've learnt yours.'

We did not have PlayStations, Nintendo 64, X-Boxes, no video games at all, no 99 channels on cable, video tape movies, surround sound, personal

cell phones, personal computers, or internet chat rooms. We made up games with sticks and tennis balls and ate worms, and although we were told it would happen, we did not put out very many eyes, nor did the worms live inside us forever.

– *Anonymous, 'People over 35 should be dead'*

Children are experts at play. They do not need to be constantly entertained by adults. Children do not require expensive toys or equipment – they have the imagination and enthusiasm to be able to play anywhere with anything. They do, however, need time. Although they may request assistance, children do not require constant adult supervision when playing. Adults can be tempted to over direct play or to control a situation when it may be in the best interests of the children to work it out themselves. Playing helps children learn to be independent. Some of the other benefits of play include:

- learning control over emotions;
- learning fairness, respect, sharing, responsibility and the consequences of your actions;
- learning to express yourself;
- learning your physical limitations.

Action 5.7
Simple resources for encouraging inside play

Drawing

- Chalk
- Blackboard
- Paints
- Pencils
- Textas
- Paper

Craft

- Scissors
- Glue
- Sticky tape
- Stapler
- Scraps of material
- Old magazines

Toys

- Blocks
- Train set
- Dolls and dolls house
- Cardboard boxes

Games

- Board games
- Twister
- Cards
- Puzzles

Play

- Dress-up box (stock up at the local op-shop)
- Dancing
- CD/tape player
- Inside cubbies (use blankets)
- Treasure box (buttons/keys/marbles/assorted household bits and pieces)

8.

Dad's dinner: Surprise picnic

It's Dad's turn to cook dinner.

But he's not cooking.

He's packing a picnic basket.

'Are we going on a picnic?' I say.

'Yes,' says Dad. 'Thought we might have a barbecue down at the beach.'

'Why?' I say.

'Why not?' says Dad. 'It's a nice night. Something different. Have a bit of a run around afterwards.'

'Cool,' I say.

Pretty soon we're standing around a barbecue in a park beside the water.

There's a warm wind blowing. I'm drinking freshly squeezed orange juice and dipping sticks of carrot in a tub of homemade cucumber and yoghurt dip.

Dad hands Mum a glass of champagne. 'This is the life!' he says, clinking glasses with her.

'What a nice surprise!' says Mum, smiling.

Dad's mobile phone rings. 'Oops,' he says, taking it out of his pocket. But he doesn't answer it. He turns it off and puts it in the picnic basket.

'What's in the packets?' says Mum, pointing to the three silver foil parcels sizzling away on the hot-plate along with some sliced potatoes and onions.

'I can't tell you,' says Dad.

'Why not?' says Mum.

'It would spoil the surprise!' he says. 'Jack, come and look after this for me, could you? I have to prepare the salad.'

Dad hands me the barbecue tongs. I flip the potatoes and move the onion rings around while Dad puts a green salad loaded with cherry tomatoes and sprouts into the middle of the table. He squeezes lemon over the top and then looks at me. 'Is it cooked, Jack?' he says.

'The potatoes and onions are,' I say. 'Don't know about the packets.'

'They'll be cooked,' says Dad. 'You can take it all off.'

I put it all on a plate and carry it across to the table.

Dad puts a packet on each of our plates.

'Okay,' he says, 'you can open them.'

'Ouch,' I say, burning my fingers on the hot foil. 'They're hot.'

'Oh yeah,' said Dad. 'I forgot to warn you. They're hot.'

'Gee, thanks Dad,' I say.

'Don't mention it!' he says.

I peel back the foil to reveal a piece of steamed fish with olive halves and spring onions on top.

'That's a work of art,' says Mum, looking at Dad with admiration. 'You're a genius!'

'It's taken you this long to realise it?' says Dad, with a look of complete amazement on his face.

An increasing amount of research over the last few years has shown that psychological and social wellbeing plays a huge role in our physical health, not just through smoking, diet and exercise, but in its own right.

– Dr Norman Swan, ABC Radio, 30 November 1998

Good health is not simply the absence of disease. A truly healthy life is a balanced life where attention is given to the mental, emotional and spiritual aspects of life as well as the physical. A balanced approach is always preferable to an obsessive concern with a particular area of your life at the expense of others, be it work, family, leisure, or even health. Perhaps one of the most powerful and long-lasting ways you can benefit your children is to model balance. You don't have to say anything – the results will do the talking for you.

Action 5.8
Taking stock

Consider each of the following five areas of your life with regard to balance. Are you giving an equal amount of attention to each of them? Or are one or two being fed at the expense of the others?

- WORK: Do you enjoy the way in which you make a living? If not, why not? What changes – either in conditions or attitude – could you make to gain more fulfilment from your work? Have you considered changing your work?
- PHYSICAL: Are you happy with your body? Are you getting regular exercise most days of the week? If not, why not? What changes could you make so that exercise could be a regular part of your life?
- SOCIAL: Family, friends and community are very important factors in our overall happiness. Do you give them the time they deserve? If not, why not? What changes could you make to rectify this?

- MENTAL: How do you keep your mind active and challenged? What are your passions? What are your interests? When did you last read a book, undertake a course of study or learn a new skill?
- SPIRITUAL: It's very easy to get caught up looking after other people and in the process neglect yourself. Do you take time out each day to nurture and renew yourself in some way? If not, why not? What changes could you make to allow this to happen?

9. Playing footy: Jack see, Jack do

After the barbecue Dad is teaching me how to do torpedo kicks.

'Not like that, Jack,' says Dad, adjusting the angle of the football in my hands.

'Okay,' I say. 'Here goes.' I drop the ball. It flies off the side of my boot and into the middle of the picnic rug.

'Hey!' says Mum, as the plates and glasses go flying.

'Oops,' I say. 'Sorry.'

'Never mind,' says Dad, running to fetch it. He brings it back and puts it into my hands. 'Try again.'

I nod.

Concentrate.

I feel the weight of the ball in my hands. The slippery surface of the still-new leather under my fingers. The smell of pine trees. The last golden shafts of the setting sun breaking through the clouds. Dad to my left.

I drop the ball straight onto my boot.

It flies through the air spinning end on end.

A perfect torpedo!

'Well done!' says Dad, running after it.

I chase him. He looks over his shoulder. 'And it's star recruit Jack coming from behind,' he narrates in mock footy commentary. 'But he's just not fast enough . . .'

The ball is just up ahead.

Dad's getting ready to dive for it.

I close in on him, tackle him around the waist and hurl him aside. I grab the ball and sprint away before he can get up off the ground.

'Be careful, Jack,' calls Mum. 'He's an old man, you know.'

'Old man?' growls Dad. 'I'll show you old man!' He takes off after me at lightning speed. I'm beginning to get a hint of what Bill was talking about when he was describing how Dad used to play.

I run as fast as I can, but Dad is faster this time.

He steals the ball straight out of my hands, keeps running the entire length of the football oval and then boots the ball through the goalposts.

He turns to me and jumps up into the air with his forefingers raised. 'GOAL!' he bellows.

I clap. 'Good one, Dad,' I say.

I don't mind.

It's good to let him win sometimes.

Keeps him interested.

Everyone should be his own physician. We ought to assist and not force nature. Eat with moderation and with what agrees with your constitution. Nothing is good for the body but what we can digest. What medicine can produce digestion? Exercise. What will recruit strength? Sleep. What will alleviate incurable ills? Patience.

– *Voltaire*

The most common reason for beginning an exercise program is the desire for a 'leaner, fitter look'. But after a few weeks of increased movement, many people realise that the secondary benefits are far greater than they could have imagined. Most people, after the initial discomfort of beginning exercise after years of not exercising, really enjoy the sense of wellbeing, decreased stress, better mental focus, better motor-skill coordination, increased confidence and better quality of life that flow from it. These become far more immediate and motivating than the leaner, fitter look that motivated them to start the program. The leaner, fitter look will certainly appear if a training program is maintained over a sustained period of time, but it is the accompanying sense of wellbeing that is perhaps the real benefit of becoming fitter. Think of the leaner, fitter look as an added bonus that will come in time, rather than it being the main point. The sense of increased wellbeing that comes with exercise can be enjoyed immediately.

Action 5.9
Taking exercise further

After a few weeks or months of maintaining a daily commitment to movement, you may be looking for new challenges or simply a little variation. You don't need to join a gym, buy expensive equipment or hire a personal trainer to do this. Try incorporating one or more of the following workouts into your weekly exercise schedule. Allow at least 24 to 48 hours to recover from a more-strenuous-than-usual session, and don't forget to perform a set of the warm-up stretches on pages 297–298 both before and after your workout.

- STRENGTH WORKOUT: For this workout you don't need anything more than a park or a backyard and a bench/seat. Perform the following series of actions which alternates between the muscles of the upper body and lower body (see the accompanying explanations and diagrams in the Sources and resources section on pages 298–300):
  - 4–6 push-ups
  - 4–6 step-ups – one set on each leg

- 4–6 tricep dips
- 4–6 squat jumps
- 4–6 sit-ups

Repeat this sequence three times. As you grow stronger you can steadily increase the number of repetitions of each exercise you perform by one each week. When you can do twelve repetitions of each exercise reasonably comfortably, you can increase the number of sets by one. Give your body a day or two to recover before repeating this workout.

- CARDIOVASCULAR WORKOUT: For this workout you need a park, beach or open grassy area. Mark out a distance between 50 and 100 metres.
  - Run at about 60 per cent of your maximum effort between your markers and then jog slowly back to the first marker, allowing yourself between 30 seconds and one minute recovery time.
  - Repeat six times. Do this high-intensity session three or four times a week, perhaps in place of a longer low-intensity session.
  - Build this up steadily over a period of time by adding an extra sprint each week up to a maximum of twelve, or an extra 10 metres of distance up to 100 metres. Ideally you should be looking at two sets of six sprints of 100 metres, each at 80 per cent of your maximum effort, with recovery time down to 30 seconds between sprints.
- CROSS-TRAINING WORKOUT: The idea of cross-training is to do a mix of both strength training and cardiovascular

training in the one session. It is a very efficient way to lose weight and increase general fitness at the same time. There are many ways to do this, but some simple methods of mixing them up include:

- Jog or skip for two to three minutes in between each set of the strength-training workout above.
- Perform one set of sprints and then do a set of the strength-training workout exercises.
- Go for a run or walk, and vary speed and intensity at random every couple of minutes, e.g. slow for two minutes, fast for one minute, slow for one minute, medium-fast for two minutes, etc.

• It is a good idea to keep an exercise diary (a cheap exercise book will do) in which you keep a record of each session, as it is very easy to lose track of how many repetitions and sets of exercises you are doing in each session.

• Some useful books that can help you to expand and vary the basic programs above are listed in the Sources and resources section on page 294.

10. Bedtime: Feeling good

At home after the barbecue, I eat a bowl of fresh strawberries in yoghurt and watch my taped episode of *Survivor*.

Somehow it's not quite as exciting as it was on the ad.

There are not quite as many crocodiles as I thought.

And nobody seems like they're in the slightest danger of being eaten. Rip-off.

I turn it off before it's even half over. I feel wrecked. But not in a '*Gee I feel lousy and I think I'm going to die*' sort of way. More of an '*I know I'm tired but my whole body is buzzing and it feels really good*' way. I dunno. It's kind of hard to explain.

I go to my bedroom.

It's a bit of a mess.

In fact there's a lot of a mess.

A football, a soccer ball, a basketball, a cricket ball, a Squidgie ball, a set of plastic wickets, kneepads, a Frisbee, a flying ring, a kite and a Totem Tennis pole. And that's just the floor.

I pick my way carefully through it all, put my new pyjamas on and go to the bathroom to brush my teeth.

I say goodnight to Mum and Dad.

'Get a good night's sleep,' says Dad. 'You're going to need it. We've got a long way to ride tomorrow.'

'What time are we starting?' I say.

'Eight o'clock,' says Dad. 'I want to try to get to Cherry Lake and back before noon. Before it gets too hot. Don't want your mother complaining.'

'Leave me out of it,' says Mum. 'You're the one who complains about getting sweat in your eyes, poor baby.'

'Whatever,' says Dad. 'We'll see.'

'Not with sweat in your eyes, you won't,' I say.

Dad winks. 'See you in the morning.'

'Night, Jack,' says Mum.

'Goodnight,' I say.

I walk to my bedroom.

I look at the floor. I know I should clean it up,

but it would take too long. It will be much quicker – and safer – to jump.

I crouch down, take a deep breath and jump from the doorway across the room to the bed. The mattress springs groan.

'Jack!' says Mum from the living room. 'Stop jumping on the bed!'

'I wasn't,' I say.

And, for once at least, it's true.

Kids understand why their parents need to work, but they don't understand why they need to work so much . . . most young people want more time with their parents rather than more money through more parental work.

– Dr Barbara Pocock and Jane Clarke, Money Can't Buy Me Love

The principles of a healthy lifestyle are not new. Neither are they particularly complicated. They involve slowing down and paying attention to our lives and the lives of our children. Paying attention to our bodies. Paying attention to what we eat. Paying attention to our lifestyle and asking ourselves whether being constantly 'busy' and always in a rush proves that we 'have a life' or is simply just a blur of mindless activity that covers up the fact that we've forgotten how to truly live. The evidence suggests that the 'fast food and no play' lifestyle is producing a vast number of unhealthy children and adults. The evidence also suggests, however, that slow food and lots of play may not only improve our health, but improve our whole quality of life. But don't take our word for it – try it for yourself.

Action 5.10
A five-point plan for restoring balance in your life

1. Stop reading this book.
2. Stand up and take a deep breath.
3. If you're hungry have a piece of fresh fruit.
4. If you're thirsty have a glass of water.
5. Go outside and take a walk. Take your children with you. Enjoy yourselves!

Action points index

PART 1

PART 2

PART 3

PART 4

PART 5

Sources and resources

QUOTATIONS

Prologue: quoted from Lazyboy, 'Underwear Goes Inside the Pants', www.LazyboyTV.com.

Page 5: quoted from 'Children's Health or Corporate Wealth: The case for banning television advertising to children', CFAC, November 2003, www.cfac.org.au.

Page 10: quoted from 'We eat too much sugar', *Herald Sun*, 24 October 2004. Courtesy of The Herald & Weekly Times Pty Ltd.

Page 15: quoted from 'How we grew so big', *Time*, 28 June 2004.

Page 21: quoted from *If Not Dieting, Then What?*, Dr Rick Kausman, page 24, Allen & Unwin, Sydney, 2004.

Page 28: quoted from *Your Active Child: How to boost physical, emotional, and cognitive development through age-appropriate activity*, Rae Pica, page 63, Contemporary Books, New York, 2003.

Page 34: quoted by Morgan Spurlock in 'Mac Daddy', *Inpress*, 2 June 2004.

Page 39: quoted by Grant Tomkinson, lecturer, School of Health Sciences, University of South Australia, in 'Parenting: Huff and Puff', *Sunday Life*, 4 July 2004.

Page 45: quoted from 'Getting to core of the matter', *Herald Sun*, 23 February 2005.

Page 51: quoted from *The Great Australian Diet: the Atkins alternative*, Dr John Tickell, page 108, Wilkinson Publishing Pty Ltd, Melbourne, 2004.

Page 57: quoted by Associate Professor Melissa Wake, Royal Children's Hospital's Centre for Community Child Health. Reproduced with kind permission.

Page 65: quoted from *French Women Don't Get Fat*, Mireille Guiliano, page 80, Chatto & Windus, London, 2005. Reprinted by permission of the Random House Group Ltd.

Page 71: quoted by Morgan Spurlock in 'Mac Daddy', *Inpress*, 2 June 2004.

Page 77: quoted from *You Are What You Eat*, Dr Gillian McKeith, page 12, Michael Joseph, London, 2004. Copyright © Celador Productions Limited, 2004. Reproduced by permission of Penguin Books Ltd.

Page 83: quoted by Rex Hunt in 'Life goes on: Rewind 1969 Rex Hunt', *Sunday Life*, 6 March 2005.

Page 90: quoted from 'Guiding Principles of the Bluearth Institute', www.bluearth.org/parents_principles.htm.

Page 98: quoted from 'Older dogs exercise minds', *Age*, 19 January 2005.

Page 104: quoted from *Fast Food Nation*, Eric Schlosser, page 43, Allen Lane, New York, 2001. Copyright © Eric Schlosser, 2001. Reproduced by permission of Penguin Books Ltd.

Page 110: quoted from *7000 Days*, Dr Reinhard W Ronnebeck, page 103, ABC Books, Sydney, 2002.

Page 116: quoted by Boyd Swinburn in The World Today: 'Childhood obesity – What's the right approach?' with Eleanor Hall, broadcast Friday 18 June 2004 on ABC Local Radio, reproduced by permission of the Australian Broadcasting Corporation and ABC Online. © 2004 ABC. All rights reserved. The full text is available at: www. abc.net.au/worldtoday/content/2004/s1135210.htm.

Page 121: quoted from *Big Fat Lies!!!: A shocking expose of the 12 biggest scams, cover-ups, lies, myths and deceptions in the diet and weight loss industries!*, Tom Venuto, a free e-book available at www.burn-the-fat.com.

Page 127: quoted from *Bridget Jones's Diary*, page 257, Helen Fielding, Macmillan Limited, London, 1996.

Page 132: quote from Margaret Fulton. Reproduced by kind permission.

Page 137: quoted from *Your Perfect Body: A state of mind*, Craig Harper, page 180, Geoff Slattery Publishing, Melbourne, 2004.

Page 142: quoted from *Play in Early Childhood*, Mary Sheridan et al, page 4, Routledge, an imprint of Taylor Francis, Oxford, 1999.

Page 148: quoted from *Your Perfect Body: A state of mind*, Craig Harper, page 88.

Page 153: quoted from *Changing Habits Changing Lives: Simple steps to rediscover health and vitality*, Cyndi O'Meara, page 98, Penguin Group Australia Ltd, Camberwell, 1999.

Page 159: quoted from *Big Fat Lies!!!*, Tom Venuto.

Page 165: adapted from 'The Difference He Made', by Randy Poole, www.inspirationpeak.com.

Page 171: quoted from *Trim for Life*, Garry Egger, page 70, Allen & Unwin, Sydney, 1997.

Page 177: quoted from *Encouraging Participation in Active Leisure*, Gary Henshall, Gary Henshall and Associates Pty Ltd, Bendigo, 2001.

Page 182: quoted by Søren Kierkegaard in a letter to *Jette*, 1847.

Page 187: quoted from 'Clinical Practice Guidelines for the Management of Overweight and Obesity in Adults', page 99, National Health and Medical Research Council, Commonwealth of Australia, 2003. Copyright © Commonwealth of Australia, reproduced by permission.

Page 194: quoted from *Our Toxic World: Who is looking after our children?*, Harold E Buttram, MD and Richard Piccola, MHA, available from Foresight/America, www.healing.org.

Page 199: quoted by Stephanie Alexander in 'Teach kids about good food and the lessons of life follow', *Age*, 13 July 2004.

Page 205: quoted by Gwendolyn Stansbury in 'Arresting Fast Food', M/C Journal 3.3 (2000), 3 May 2005, http://journal.media-culture.org.au/0006/food.php.

Page 210: quoted by Mireille Guiliano in 'Saying oui to a little pleasure', *Age*, 15 January 2005.

Page 214: quoted from *Fast Food Nation*, Eric Schlosser, page 269.

Page 219: quoted by Glenn Harrison of Melbourne, Australia on www.aerobie.com.

Page 225: quoted from *The Obesity Myth*, Paul Campos, page 245, Viking, 2004. Copyright © 2004 Paul Campos. Used by permission of Gotham Books, an imprint of Penguin Group (USA) Inc.

Page 229: quoted from *Light, Medicine of the Future*, J Liberman, page 58, Bear & Co., Santa Fe, 1991.

Page 233: quoted by Phillip Adams (source unknown).

Page 239: quoted from *The Healing Power of Sleep*, Sheila Lavery, page 9, Gaia Books, Sussex, 1997.

Page 243: adapted from 'All I Want for Christmas . . . Parents, you may be surprised', Linda Sharp, author of *Stretchmarks On My Sanity*, www.sheknows.com.

Page 247: quoted from 'People over 35 should be dead' (author unknown).

Page 252: quoted from *Your Active Child*, Rae Pica, pages 63–64.

Page 257: quoted by Dr David Ludwig, director of the obesity program at Boston's Children's Hospital, in 'The Obesity Warriors', *Time*, 28 June 2004.

Page 262: quoted from *Your Active Child*, Rae Pica, page 145.

Page 266: quoted from 'People over 35 should be dead' (author unknown).

Page 271: quoted by Dr Norman Swan in 'Mastering the Control Factor', *The Health Report*, ABC Radio National, 30 November 1998.

Page 276: quoted by Voltaire.

Page 282: quoted from *Money Can't Buy Me Love: Young Australians' views of parental work, time, guilt and their own consumption*, Barbara Pocock & Jane Clarke, The Australia Institute, 2004.

RECOMMENDED RESOURCES

If you've been inspired by this book to pursue a healthier lifestyle – or simply to find out more information – the following books and websites are highly recommended.

Books

Dr John Tickell, *The Great Australian Diet: The Atkins alternative*, Wilkinson Publishing Pty Ltd, Melbourne, 2004.

Simple and extremely practical guide to sustainable weight loss and increased energy. The perfect next step for anyone serious about creating a healthier lifestyle. For more information visit: www.drjohntickell.com.

Craig Harper, *Your Perfect Body: A state of mind*, Geoff Slattery Publishing, Melbourne, 2004.

How to cultivate the right attitude to help you to look better, feel better and be more in control of your body. Includes many helpful case studies of ordinary people who've made big changes.

Dr Rick Kausman, *If Not Dieting, Then What?*, Allen & Unwin, Sydney, 2004.

A thorough non-dieting approach to healthy weight management. More information and useful tip sheets at www.ifnotdieting.com.

Mireille Guiliano, *French Women Don't Get Fat*, Chatto & Windus, New York, 2005.

Part memoir, part guide to how to live a disciplined but pleasure-filled life.

Rae Pica, *Your Active Child: How to boost physical, emotional, and cognitive development through age-appropriate activity*, Contemporary Books, New York, 2003.

This comprehensive book explains why children need to move and is packed with activities to get them moving.

Eric Schlosser, *Fast Food Nation*, Allen Lane, New York, 2001.

Everything you ever wanted to know about every aspect of the fast food industry . . . and plenty that you didn't.

Greg Critser, *Fat Land: How Americans became the fattest people in the world*, Allen Lane, London, 2003.

A detailed study of the many factors of modern life

that have converged to make 60 per cent of the American population overweight.

Websites

www.healthyactive.gov.au

Australian Government website that provides many links to practical advice on how children, young people and families can be more physically active and choose healthy foods.

www.nutritionaustralia.org

Nutrition Australia aims to provide scientifically based nutrition information to encourage all Australians to achieve optimal health through food variety and physical activity.

www.parentsjury.org.au

A web-based network of parents who wish to improve the food and physical activity environments for children in Australia.

www.supersizeme.com

Supersize Me is a powerful documentary that has brought widespread attention to the epidemic of obesity. Essential viewing for anyone who has ever eaten – or is contemplating eating – fast food.

www.bluearth.org

Programs and information facilitating the development and integration of mind, body and spirit through participation in physical activity.

WARM-UP STRETCHES

Before you start a mini-circuit it is an excellent idea to warm up with ten to fifteen minutes of brisk walking and stretching. Even if you're not doing a mini-circuit, it's great to do a stretching session each day.

Seated gluteus and hip stretch
Sit on the ground with both legs extended. Pull the right leg underneath your left leg until it is at a right angle. Put your left hand on the floor for balance and then hug your knee with your right arm and pull in towards your chest. Hold the stretch for 10–20 seconds. Then change legs. Repeat two to three times.

Tricep and deltoid stretch
Standing up straight, place one hand just above the elbow of one arm. Gently pull the upper arm towards your chest. Hold for 10–20 seconds. Switch sides. Repeat two to three times.

Soleus (lower calf) stretch
Put your arms against a wall at right angles. Place one leg in front of the other leg. Keeping your feet flat on the ground, bend your knees in towards the wall until you can feel the stretch in the lower part of your rear leg. Hold for 10–20 seconds. Switch to the other leg. Repeat two to three times.

Lying hamstring stretch

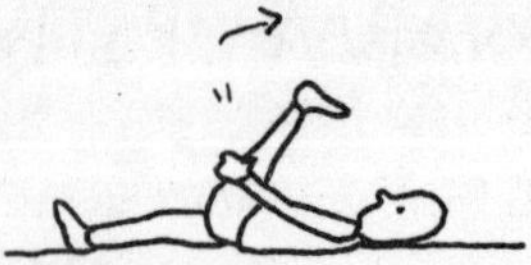

Lie on your back with your legs straight. Raise one leg. Clasp your hands behind the thigh of this leg just below the knee. Try to bring the thigh as close to your chest as possible while keeping the leg straight. Repeat with the other leg. Repeat two to three times.

Quadricep stretch

Lie on your side. Keeping your bottom leg straight, bend your knee so that you can grasp the ankle of the top leg. Gently pull the heel of this leg towards your bottom. Hold for 10–20 seconds. Switch to the other leg. Repeat two to three times.

STRENGTH WORKOUT: MINI-CIRCUIT

Push-ups

This exercise uses shoulders, chest and triceps.

Beginner push-up: Kneel down on the ground and cross your feet over. Place your hands in front of your body, a little bit in front of the shoulders. Lower yourself down towards the floor and push yourself back up again.

Full push-up: Kneel down on the ground with your hands out in front of your body. Raise yourself up onto your toes. Lower yourself down to the ground and then push straight back up again. Try not to let your bottom drop.

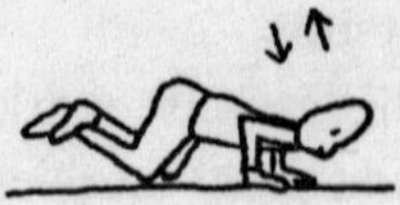

Step-ups

Great exercise for toning the legs – it uses quadriceps, hamstrings and gluteus maximus (bottom).

Find a stable bench or chair. Put one foot on the chair. Raise yourself up until your leg is fully extended. Then lower yourself back down. Repeat four to six times on this leg and then change legs.

Tricep dips

This exercise works your tricep muscle.

Find a stable bench or chair. Facing away from the bench, place both hands behind you. Grip the bench with arms touching the sides of your body and your legs at right angels. Lower your body until your upper arms are nearly horizontal and then push yourself back up to the starting position.

Sit-ups

This exercise works your abdominal muscles.

Lie with your knees bent and your feet flat on the ground. Fold your arms across your chest. Raise your upper body until you can feel your stomach muscles contract. Hold the contraction for a count of three and then go back to the starting position.

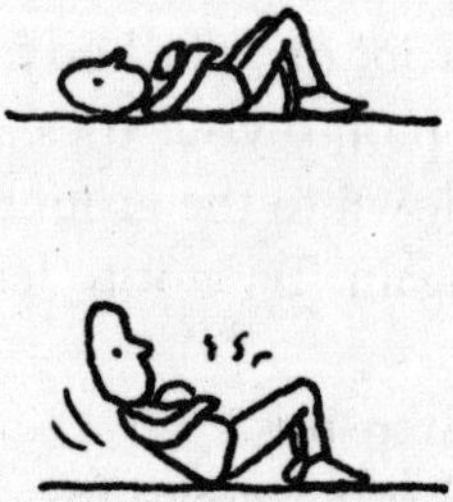

Squat jumps

This exercise works the quadriceps, glutes and hamstrings.

Crouch down until your legs are at right angles to the ground. Place your hands in front of you for balance and then using your legs, jump as high as you can. Return to your starting position and repeat.